SMALL-GROUP LEADER'S

QUICK
GUIDE

to *(Almost)* Everything

Syler Thomas & Steven Tighe

SMALL-GROUP LEADER'S
QUICK GUIDE
to *(Almost)* Everything

Copyright © 2020 Syler Thomas/0000 0001 1218 4773 and
Steven Tighe/0000 0004 8388 1105
Visit our website: **group.com**

Authors: Syler Thomas and Steven Tighe
Editor: Rick Lawrence
Chief Creative Officer: Joani Schultz
Copy Editor: Lyndsay Gerwing
Art Director: Darrin Stoll
Marketing Manager: Karen Hennings

Real. **Bold.** Love.

ISBN 978-1-4707-5964-3
Epub 978-1-4707-5965-0
Printed in the United States of America.
10 9 8 7 6 5 4 3 2 1   29 28 27 26 25 24 23 22 21 20

Table of Contents

Introduction

Where we tell you who we are and why you should read this book...

Welcome, small-group leader!

Ministry to teenagers is crazy important. That's why we wrote this book. We're passionate about helping small-group leaders (like you) learn how to be transformational influencers. As we wrote this guide, we pictured ourselves sitting with you around a table piled with coffee cups and giant apple fritters the size of dinner plates. Likely someone gave you this book because you're leading, or have been asked to lead, a small group. We want you to know that what you're doing (or preparing to do) is vital and eternal. In just a minute we'll tell you why. But first, introductions...

Who are we?

We're both youth ministers, and we've known each other for a long time. In fact, as a teenager Syler was in a small group that Steven led. Here's the bedtime-version story of how we became friends and eventually partners in ministry...

Once upon a time, there was a young engineer named Steven. He'd just moved to Austin, Texas, for his first job and knew no one, so he joined a close-by church to meet people. The church was full of people his age, and they were some of the friendliest, coolest-seeming people he'd ever met. Except for one thing. They talked about Jesus all the time. Steven grew up in church, but he'd never heard people talk, much less joke, about Jesus. At first Steven tried to talk them out of the whole Jesus thing, but he gradually came to realize that the Jesus they talked and joked about was actually worth giving up his life to follow. Shortly after that revelation, he started helping them lead the church's youth group. This is where Steven's and Syler's stories connect.

Once upon a time, there was a boy named Syler. His family attended the same church that Steven had just joined. Syler got involved with the youth group, and when he was a senior, Steven asked him to join a team of senior highers who helped lead the middle school youth group. That ended up changing Syler's life. Here's a photo of that leadership team—with Syler on the left and Steven on the right—from December of 1990 (self-timer; there were no selfies back then).

Syler wanted to be an actor, so he headed off to Chicago to attend a school with a great drama program. He had no intention of ever serving in ministry, so it's sort of hard to explain why he graduated and then entered seminary. In seminary he had *zero* intention of ever going into youth ministry, but when he graduated, the best offer he got was a youth pastor job. He took it, then accidently fell in love with youth ministry, then kept at it for 20 years and counting.

In the meantime, Steven, who had no intention of leaving his well-paid job in engineering, inexplicably decided to move to Pittsburgh to take a position teaching youth ministry at a denominational seminary. Since then he has been working with teenagers and training the people who serve them, and he and Syler have stayed pretty close (in fact, most of the youth group they were a part of has stayed pretty close).

And one day, over deep-dish Chicago pizza, Syler and Steven (the two friends who seemed least likely ever to work with teenagers—maybe like you?) decided to write a book.

There. That catches us up.

And now, in case you're unsure that you have what it takes to be a small-group leader, let's put your mind at ease.

Good places to shop for the skinny jeans all youth workers must have... (by Steven)

We can picture what typical youth workers are supposed to look like. They're young, fun, and hip—and teenagers seem naturally drawn to them. A lot of people never even consider working with teenagers because they don't think they fit that impossible description.

Here's the good news: You can relax. The majority of people who work effectively with teenagers are none of these things, and you don't need to be, either (as Syler would tell you, I've been young but never hip). Serving with teenagers isn't like being back in high school—you don't need to dress a certain way or act a certain way or worry about your relative hip-ness. You need only three things to be an effective small-group leader:

1) Love Jesus.
2) Care about teenagers.
3) Be willing to build and invest your time in a relationship with them.

It turns out that one of the things kids need most is older people who genuinely care about them, and *you* already care or you wouldn't be reading this book. My friend Luke leads a small group in a Canadian church. If I asked him to share his story, he'd tell you he doesn't fit the "typical youth worker" template. Nevertheless, a few years ago, he was asked to consider discipling the teenagers in his church. Despite his serious misgivings *("I'm an introvert. The thought of spending time with young people feels overwhelming. Do we even speak the same language?"),* he started meeting with a group of students. The result has been a small, thriving, close-knit community. Luke explains, "It turns out that young people can smell 'care' under layers of nerd."

If you love Jesus and can invest a couple of hours a week giving teenagers what they so desperately need, you have everything it takes to lead a thriving small group. Our goal is to help you learn how to do that.

Polite youth ministry versus transformational discipleship...
(by Syler)

Here's the thing: There are thousands of small groups in the world, but not all of them are thriving. In a lot of groups, you'll find teenagers content to go through the motions. They show up for a couple of hours a week, they're generally well-behaved, and they sort of participate—in a word, they are...*polite.*

"Polite" perfectly describes the environment of my first (and, it turns out, my only) youth ministry position. The kids were nice and well-behaved and Christian-y. But no one was opening up about their struggles or actually showing their real selves to each other. Their primary friend groups were outside the ministry. The church youth group was just this thing they did for a couple of hours a week that had no connection to the rest of their lives. And I felt the same way—I knew this church position was just a brief roadside attraction on the way to what I was really called to do.

And then we went on a weeklong mission trip to Mexico, and everything changed.

Walls came down, people opened up, and that atmosphere of manufactured politeness melted away. Stuff got real. I laughed harder that week than I had in years. And Jesus showed up. I can't point to a single moment that week and declare, "There—that's when it happened." Simply, over the course of a challenging week, a group of teenagers and adult leaders grew in their fondness for each other, fueled by the power of the Holy Spirit. We lost our facades, and because of that our lives changed as we pursued Jesus together. When we returned home, the "Mexico Breakthrough" transformed our ministry environment. These students now cared passionately for each other, understood Jesus in a whole new way, and began inviting their friends into that community.

A similar transformation happened in my high school youth group. Until my senior year, I was part of a thriving ministry full of wonderful people. But while others in the group were growing as disciples, I maintained a polite distance. In my senior year, after Steven asked me to help lead the middle school youth group, my life changed. Because of my new role, Steven met weekly with me and two other high school leaders. We studied the Bible together, worshipped together, and prayed together. All of this forced my focus off myself and onto others, and I began to understand what it meant to be a disciple.

If the best we can hope for is "polite" youth ministry, then honestly, what's the point? Jesus is calling us to join him in making disciples, not polite churchgoers. The goal of any effective youth ministry is *transformational* discipleship, and it most often happens in the context of a small group. When your ministry environment encourages life-on-life mentoring as you pursue Jesus together, the fruit is profound. You get young people who sacrificially love one another, who care for the forgotten and marginalized, and who live not for their own glory but for God's.

None of this happens by accident. So in the pages that follow, we'll walk you through the milestones that have marked our own journey and show you how to "prepare the soil" of your ministry environment for the kind of growth that produces Jesus-size fruit.

Transformational discipleship changes the world... (back to Steven)

Transformational discipleship isn't just a goal for teenagers; it's Jesus' goal for his whole church. But if it's a goal for all Christians, why do we need a book that talks about how small groups transform teenagers into disciples? Well, because kids need special attention!

First, a staggering fact: Adolescents are more open to the Gospel than they will be at any other point in their lives. This is not that surprising when you consider that the teenage years are the setting for most of the big decisions we make in life—the people we're going to spend our lives with, the choice of a career path, and yes, what "religious" path we'll follow. According to a 2019 study by Ministry-to-Children.com, those who have not committed their lives to Jesus by their 21st birthday have only a 16 percent chance of ever doing it. Transformational discipleship is important for teenagers because that's when the majority of humans come to Christ.

Second, Jesus singles out young people for special attention. In Luke 18:16, some parents are trying to bring their kids to Jesus, but the disciples stop them. Jesus sharply rebukes them for keeping the children away. In Luke 17:2, Jesus uses some strong language to describe the consequences of misleading a young person: "It would be better to be thrown into the sea with a millstone hung around your neck." A millstone is huge and heavy; swimming with one tied around your neck guarantees a rapid descent to the seabed. And then there's John 21, where Jesus asks Peter three times if he loves him, responding to Peter's first response by urging him to "feed my lambs." In the following responses, Jesus changes his imperative to "feed my sheep." It sure sounds like Jesus is trying to emphasize something with Peter: First go to the young (lambs), then focus on the older (sheep). Jesus is feisty when it comes to young people and their faith. And so are we.

Third, it's important because it's hard to be a teenager. The chances of teenagers permanently damaging their lives before they reach the age of 21 are high. Opioid addiction has become an epidemic, especially among young people. Researchers say widespread addiction to smartphones, social media, and a consumer mindset is producing the most anxiety-ridden and depressed generation in U.S. history. Suicide has eclipsed homicide as the number-two killer of teenagers and is growing at an alarming rate (accidental death is the number-one killer of teenagers). Altogether it's a pretty scary picture. Young people need all the help they can get, and youth ministry can be a powerful guardrail. Syler has a friend who compares effective youth ministry to time travel: You're reaching into the past to stop life-mistakes before they happen.

We hope by now you understand that what you're doing is important. Not only does the gift of your presence matter to teenagers and their families, but it matters to the church and to Jesus. We want to help you figure out how to do it well.

Before you get to the rest of the book, a warning is probably appropriate. We get pretty passionate about working with teenagers and are apt to frequently talk as though something is the MOST IMPORTANT THING IN THE WORLD. Stay calm. You can't do everything in this book perfectly. That's okay. If some of it is useful, use it. If not, don't worry about it.

One last thing before you turn the page and get going! You know how films sometimes include a little bonus scene at the end? We like those, so we've done something similar at the end of each chapter—a "Chapter Coda" (a coda is something tacked on to the end of something). You'll find stories, poems, quotes, and even a recipe for Syler's world-famous pumpkin bread. Which is nice.

How to Be a Great Small-Group Leader

(by Steven)

In the introduction I touched on the story of how my life changed when I joined the church that Syler's family attended. But I left out some important details. I was first attracted to the church when I saw, firsthand, how much others my age were enjoying each other. I was surprised by their open, welcoming attitude toward me, even though I was a little put off by how much they talked about God. I started spending more and more time with them and eventually discovered that most of them were serving as volunteers in the church's youth group.

My first visit to the youth group was mind-blowing—one of the profound turning points of my life. I'd never seen a group of teenagers who were so affectionate with one another. They laughed all the time. They sang worship songs unselfconsciously, with energy and vulnerability. They hugged but not awkwardly. They were curious and polite to strangers (like me). The whole group—adults and teenagers— genuinely enjoyed each other. The energy in the room was magnetic. I was smitten. I had no idea what was going on, but I wanted to be a part of whatever it was.

I didn't know it then, but Jesus knew exactly what was going on in that group: "Your love for one another will prove to the world that you are my disciples" (John 13:35). Of course, I'd seen this verse before, but I hadn't experienced it as a real thing. I assumed Jesus was giving us a kind of warning, like "Treat each other well so strangers don't think Christians are jerks." But in this youth group, I discovered that people who love each other the way Jesus is describing create an irresistible community. It's impossible to see it and not want to be part of it, right? Is this not every person's secret dream—to finally find a group of people who love you and enjoy you for who you are, without posturing or deceit? Where people actually love you like Jesus loves you?

These young people and the adults who led them created a relational space that invited the Spirit of Jesus to thrive and move. They became "living stones" (1 Peter 2:4). And when a group is under the influence of the Holy Spirit, a ragtag collection of broken people morphs into a visceral experience of the body of Christ. Collectively, the group acts like Jesus acts. And that changes everything.

Soon I started volunteering, and eventually I led the group. Dozens of young people came, got involved, and met Jesus. It has shaped my entire life since then. This chapter is about what I saw in those teenagers and how, by the grace of God, we can become the kind of people who shape a group like that. And as Syler and I prayed about the message of this book, our passion for conveying the reality and power of loving, compelling, Jesus-centered relationships bubbled to the surface. There is unsurpassed redemptive power in a healthy small group; when the relationships are intimate and infused by the Spirit, nothing is more life-changing.

Why Are Relationships So Important?

As biblical Christians, we believe in one God. We don't hold to a pantheistic view like the Greeks or Romans or Hindus. At the same time, we know from the Bible that God is "triune"—he is the Father (Matthew 11:25), the Son (John 1:1), and the Spirit (John 14:26). So when we talk about the "one true God," we're referencing the Father, Son, and Holy Spirit—God is in relationship with himself. He is somehow mysteriously, miraculously, one... But the three distinct Persons experience total unity with one another, an eternal braid of affection and unity of will.

It sounds funny to say, but the Father, Son, and Holy Spirit *like each other*. They delight in one another. They enjoy their relationship and love working together. And Scripture tells us that God created us to enjoy the Three-in-One the same way they delight in each other. We've been invited into their eternal joy and delight! This invitation into joy is scattered throughout the Bible—in Psalm 16:5-11 and Philippians 4:4 for starters. But one of my favorite versions of this invitation is embedded in the Westminster confession: "The chief end of man is to glorify God and enjoy him forever." The Father, Son, and Holy Spirit enjoy each other, and as we commit ourselves in relationship with God, we are invited into their joyful affection.

In his John 14 prayer, Jesus pines for a relationship with us that mirrors the way he and the Father are one. He wants the rich, affectionate relationship that is at the center of the Trinity to flow into every crack and crevice of his kingdom—and into every ministry environment.

Jesus not only models what a rich, joyful, loving relationship looks like, but he often focuses on it with his followers. So he upgrades the Second Great Commandment—"Love your neighbor as yourself"—with a new commandment—"Love one another as I have loved you." And he spends most of his time shaping his 12 friends into a family, a community, that reflects the intimate relationships enjoyed by the Trinity. He's fashioning a fitting vessel for the Holy Spirit to inhabit after he leaves the earth.

In the same way that Jesus is seeding community among his disciples, we make rich, affectionate relationships a high priority in our small groups. It's central to our "job description"—to love our teenagers with the kind of care and attention that encourages them to form close relationships with each other. We do that by making our love for Jesus primary; out of our vertical intimacy flows horizontal intimacy. And that's an important reminder: Our small group doesn't belong to us; it belongs to Jesus. We're only taking care of it for him.

WWJD?

You know those WWJD bracelets? They reference the famous book by Charles Sheldon *In His Steps.* WWJD stands for What Would Jesus Do? It's a reminder to always consider what Jesus would do in any situation, before we speak or act (and screw things up).

Maybe those bracelets seems cheesy to you, but from a broad perspective, the concept is a helpful reminder for every ministry leader: Jesus is our "way, truth, and life." Whenever we make a decision, before we react to a problem, and prior to writing our discussion questions, we reconnect to Jesus and consider the "lean" of his heart in that situation. But it's hard to mull what Jesus would do in our disparate circumstances if we know very little about him. And so the Bible is a primary way we come to know him; we prioritize the stories about him in the four Gospels. We study the way he treats his disciples, his enemies, and authority figures. We watch how he enters into challenges and pay attention to the strategies he used to transform lives. We let Jesus teach us who he is and what he does; we don't saddle him with our assumptions and preconceived notions. We invite him to model for us how to lead a small group.

Jesus already has plans and dreams and goals for our teenagers, so we pray to join him in his mission in their lives. We plead for him to draw them to himself. We seek his plans and commit ourselves to help bring his plans into reality.

Your Main Purpose as a Small-Group Leader

If we're leading our small group as an extension of Jesus, it makes sense to ask what his purpose for the group is. We'll talk more about this in the chapter on how to plan a healthy small group, but for now let's address this central question: "What is my mission as a small-group leader?"

In the spirit of WWJD, our big question is, "What does Jesus most want for the kids in this small group?" Well, we already know he's longing for them to love him and follow him into a relationship defined by joy and fruitfulness. So that's our main goal: to guide teenagers into a deeper relationship with Jesus and form them into a community that the Holy Spirit can live inside.

I know that sounds like a huge, daunting job, but don't worry. Jesus does most of the hard work here. And as a committed adult Christian, you already have the gifts and skills you need for this job. Here's how to get started…

The Three Key Relationships for Excellent Small-Group Leaders

Guided by Jesus and his Word, effective small-group leaders focus on three relationships: 1) our relationship with Jesus, 2) our relationships with other leaders, 3) our relationships with teenagers. We'll slow down and walk through each one.

Relationship 1: Our Relationship With Jesus

I know you already know this, but it's important enough that it needs to be repeated. Your own personal relationship with Jesus will influence the students you work with more than anything else you do, teach, or say. This is not Christian-y hype; it's the simple truth.

Discipling relationships have a supernatural dynamic rooted in the Rabbi/Talmid relationship that was common in Jesus' time—the people under your care and guidance become like you. This works apart from and sometimes in opposition to what you say and teach. This is one of the reasons the Jewish authorities could tell that Jesus' disciples had been with him (Acts 4:13); the longer they were with him, the more like him they became.

- **Always be growing in your relationship with Jesus.** The best way we can help the kids in our small group is to make sure we prioritize our own deepening passion for Jesus. At one time, I strongly encouraged everyone in my small group to spend time daily praying and reading the Bible. I'd make those habits one of the conditions for leadership. Every time we met, I'd have kids report on how they were doing. But I don't do this anymore...

Years later, when one of the teenagers from that original leadership group and her husband started leading the youth group, I was shocked to discover she wasn't teaching and encouraging kids to spend regular time with Jesus. She told me that she felt so much pressure to maintain a "quiet time" in her teenage years that it had destroyed her affection for Jesus. My prerequisite for leadership had morphed into a performance imperative, another must-do on a long list of rules designed to make God happy. She didn't want that to happen to her kids.

I felt doubly terrible. First, I saw how my well-intentioned efforts to promote a deepening relationship with Jesus had degraded into legalism. Second, I was dismayed that this gifted young leader, hurt by my error, was doing little to encourage her kids to develop intentional relational habits with Jesus.

This was a tipping point for me. We can't make following Jesus seem like checking boxes on a to-do list. The point is not the list but the relationship. Now instead of requiring the practice of daily time with Jesus, I ask my teenagers and volunteers to commit to growing their intimacy with Jesus. Sometimes that means daily Bible reading; sometimes that means daily worship; sometimes that means stopping to hash something out with him (time with Jesus doesn't always have to involve the Bible). The idea is to make sure that intimacy with Jesus, not our spiritual performance, is the goal. I still check up on my teenagers and hold them accountable for their commitment, but now the point is Jesus, not going through the motions.

- **Deal with your own sin.** I mentioned the spiritual dynamic that forms students into the image of their leaders and teachers. The wrong lesson to draw from this observation is that since we all sin, none of us should lead or teach teenagers (although if you've understood the implications, it's pretty normal to be wary of "modeling sin"). The right lesson is that the kids in our small group will learn to handle sin the way we do. If we hide and defend our sin or try to appear perfect, so will they. If we live inauthentically, we will raise up young people who are gifted hypocrites. That's one of those millstone hazards. (Note: "Not hiding our sin" does *not* mean we use our small group as a confessional. We must be mature and wise about when, where, and why we share our struggles. Our goal must be to help, not to get our own needs met.)

Leaders serving in the kingdom of God must handle our own sin in a biblical way—with great humility, appropriate confession, and intentional repentance. That's what I want my teenagers to absorb from me. I want them to become eager repenters, always aware that they are broken and in need of Jesus.

- **Invite a mentor or spiritual director to guide you.** We strongly suggest that small-group leaders find a spiritual mentor, sometimes called a spiritual director or a "soul friend." This is a person who can act as a sounding board, a spiritual guide, and an important source of accountability as we do the important work of loving and nurturing our teenagers into Christian maturity.

So this is the challenge for those of us who enter into the adventure of Christian leadership. For the sake of the kids who are ingesting what you're modeling, do what it takes to grow in your intimacy with Jesus.

Relationship 2: Our Relationships With Other Leaders

If Jesus wants the Trinity's affection, respect, and love to flavor all our relationships, that will include other ministry leaders (and our lead youth pastor, if that's our situation). These relationships influence the quality of the relationships in our small group. Like our relationship with Jesus and our relationships with teenagers, close community with other leaders does not happen by accident; it must be consciously and consistently nurtured. In the kingdom of God, the people we do things with are just as important as what we're doing.

Of course, it's easy to maintain unity when things are working well, but our real differences guarantee tension. And I can't say I love other leaders but sweep our differences under the rug (an efficient way to raise up hypocrites). Instead, we exercise our courage and learn how to enjoy, respect, and value others in spite of our differences. This is the Jesus way, and it's not easy. Three practices have helped me with this:

1) When I discover that I'm having trouble with another leader, I commit to praying for that person every day. It's hard for me to stay irritated with someone I'm praying for.

2) I've made a spiritual discipline out of spending regular time with the people I have the most trouble with.

3) I practice relational hygiene...

Paradoxically, the closer a group of people grows, the easier it is for us to hurt one another. The devil, who is real, loves this. He will work to carefully nurture resentments, unforgiveness, and irritations into irreconcilable vendettas. And once a rift starts between adult leaders, it's not hard to see how it begins to divide the group. Teenagers pick up on things like that quickly, and they inevitably start picking sides. A minor misunderstanding that goes unresolved morphs into a dramatic division between quickly forming cliques.

This is why it's important to practice Ephesians 4:26 wisdom—we must take care of relational issues quickly: "Don't sin by letting anger control you. Don't let the sun go down while you are still angry, for anger gives a foothold to the devil." I call this "flossing your friendships." In the same way we use dental floss to pry the junk out of our teeth so they stay healthy, we drag our feelings of hurt, resentment, and anger into the light so we can maintain healthy relationships.

The practical implication is that our personal issues need to be handled quickly. We can't afford to let frustrations or resentments simmer. If we don't take care of trouble spots quickly, they fester and grow into relational cancer. The devil will use this foothold to damage the relationships in your group.

For example, I like to joke around with other leaders. But many times, usually at the end of a long trip when everyone is exhausted, someone has hurt my feelings by pushing the envelope with their humor. I usually don't realize that I've been hurt until I catch myself getting angry inside, contemplating ways to hurt them or get back at them. It is *so* hard to stop in the moment, go to that person, and confess that what they said hurt me. It's embarrassing and humiliating, but I've discovered the hard way that letting resentment fester is always worse.

The best way to teach relational hygiene to my students is to practice it with other leaders, and with them. Which brings us to…

Relationship 3: Our Relationships With Teenagers

What does it mean to form close relationships with teenagers? Imagine what some adult could've done for you when you were their age, and figure out how to do that for your teenagers.

- **Show up.** Obviously, there are limits on how and when you spend time with kids (we'll focus more on that in our chapter on boundaries). And yes, even though we're building close friendships with them, we still must mete out discipline and hold them accountable for their words and actions. We're adults, not peers. They need someone older and wiser who can listen to them and show them how important they are to Jesus by taking them seriously. That means spending our time and attention on them. In a sense, as an adult you have a built-in superpower: *You're older.* For teenagers, one of the most precious resources in the universe is the attention of an older person who cares for them.

The first step in caring is simply showing up. In a society where adults, and especially parents, fill up their margins with busyness and divorce rates are sky-high, an adult who consistently chooses to be with them is countercultural—and a profound illustration of the Father's love. As simple as it seems, the commitment we make to be there for our kids underscores the passion of the Incarnation. God becomes man, just to *be with* us.

• **Be a "relational pillar" for healthy faith.** In Chapter 8: "How to Understand Adolescence, and Why It Matters," we focus on the "Relational Pillars of Adolescent Faith": Christian peers, Christian mentors, and direct experiences of Jesus. As small-group leaders, we become one of these crucial pillars. Our role as Christian mentors supports and builds kids' faith. Of course, we aren't their only mentors. But their access to other ministry leaders is often limited. They'll spend way more time with us than with our church's lead pastor or youth pastor. Time, caring, and conversation are absolutely vital! It's in close relationships with caring adults that real life-change happens. So remember, the way we relate to our teenagers matters. They're trying to figure out if they're as loved by God as we say they are and if there's a place for them in the kingdom of God. Ideally, our community environment will be so infused with encouragement, respect, joy, and honest truth that every teenager will be "infected" by the love of God.

A Challenge and a Request

If we shape our small group into a community of people who love each other the way Jesus loved his disciples, it will change their lives forever. So here is our challenge: Pursue that dream with your group. Decide now that you're going to do whatever it takes to "fertilize" the environment in your group with close relationships, enriching the soil so that growth is organic.

And here's our request: First and always, invite Jesus to be involved in this. Pray now, and pray every day, for the teenagers in your group—that they will fall in love with Jesus and learn to love one another the way he does. Plead with him to shape the relationships in your group so that whenever outsiders see your kids together, they know your kids follow Jesus.

CHAPTER CODA

Syler and I both lead worship. Sometimes when the mood strikes, we make up songs. (It's too lofty to say we write them.) One day Syler and I were waiting for our middle school students to arrive. We were laughing about how people say they hear God's "still, small voice" even though his voice in the Bible is usually huge, loud, and unmistakable. So we started singing about God speaking to Noah, Pharaoh, and Jonah. And that experiment turned into a song that we called "Subtle as a Truck." Here are the lyrics to the first verse and the chorus. Note that you must pronounce the silent "b" in the first "subtle" in the chorus. That's important. Later we took our small group into a studio and recorded it (a GREAT group activity, by the way). You can listen to the recording by searching for "Subtle as a Truck" on YouTube.com.

Let's talk about Noah, and the people in his land.
They were bad. God got mad.
And God said repent, but they didn't.
So God sent a flood, and they all drowned.

CHORUS
Oh Lord, that's subtle. Subtle as a truck.
Driving at your face, crashing through your door.
Hard to ignore (beep beep!).
Oh Lord, that's subtle. Subtle as a truck.

For the verses about Pharaoh and Jonah, check it out on YouTube.com!

How to Plan a Great Small Group

(by Syler)

A friend invited Bob to our winter retreat, but he really had no idea what he was getting himself into. He was into snowboarding, so he liked that part of it. He was assigned to my small group that weekend but didn't talk much. He was your average, apathetic teenage boy, and when the retreat was over, I didn't think we'd ever see him again. To close out the final small-group gathering of the retreat, I had everyone hold hands. I told them I'd start with a prayer, then squeeze the hand of the person next to me. If you didn't want to pray, you could just squeeze the next person's hand—no pressure at all. When the hand-squeezing got to Bob, I figured he would "opt out" and keep the squeeze moving. He didn't. But he didn't pray, either. Instead, he sort of addressed the group: "Hey, just wanted you guys to know that I've had a good time, and I appreciate everything I've learned, and uh, yeah, take care."

In essence, he prayed…to us. Bob was *so awkward*. And genuine. And wonderful. And to my great surprise, Bob came to youth group the next week. And the next. He signed up for our summer mission trip, where he gave his life to Jesus. Six years later, I had the privilege of officiating at his wedding. He married a young woman he'd met at youth group (she'd also been invited by a friend). Now my kids are his kids' babysitters.

And it all started with an awkward experience in a small group.

Why does it have to be so awkward? This is one of the great mysteries of life, on par with "Why did God choose to create all this in the first place?" and "Why do we shiver sometimes when we pee?" Some mysteries will never be solved. But it's no mystery that when we invest ourselves in small groups, lives change.

In this chapter, we'll highlight what you can do *before* your small group to make the experience as effective as possible. In the next chapter we'll focus on what you can do *during* the small-group experience to maximize its impact. The goal, again, is to move from polite youth ministry to transformational discipleship. This never happens by accident. Strong relationships are born out of close-knit community, not simply "hangout time." In a close community, the members know each other well, love doing life together, and are committed to encouraging and challenging one another.

On the Other Side of Awkward Is Awesome

I was speaking to the parents of incoming freshmen, warning them that it was quite possible they'd hear their kids complaining about an awkward small-group experience at some point in the future. Most small groups start out awkward because, simply, the kids don't know each other. But the last thing they should do at that point is give up. You know why? If they can push through the awkward phase (and then the phrase just came to me)...

"On the other side of awkward is awesome."

Catchy, right?

So how do we get there?

Well, first there are some decisions that need to be made about your group. The first involves what kind of group you have.

I have a friend who leads a small group of middle school students during a Sunday morning service, but her leaders (the youth pastor and children's pastor) have never really clarified the group's purpose. The youth pastor assumed the obvious purpose was relational connection, and the children's pastor assumed the obvious purpose was to teach the Bible. So neither one ever clarified their assumptions—that means my friend got contradictory, unclear input. She spent a semester just kind of hanging out with the kids. I want to highlight two important lessons here:

1. Small groups can have a wide variety of useful purposes.

2. Any group without a clear purpose will inevitably devolve into teenagers simply talking about themselves with each other.

Your Group Needs a Purpose

The group I joined during my senior year in high school was a **leadership group**. Yes, we shared our lives and prayed for one another. We worshipped together and studied the Bible. But the main purpose of the group was to lead the church's middle schoolers, so we did a lot of training, planning, and evaluation. All those other things simply helped us better minister to those kids.

For example, all small groups include sharing, but some make **sharing** the main purpose. Steven leads a post-college internship program at his church. His interns are involved in part-time jobs and ministries, so the main thing they need is a time to touch-base with each other. They don't study the Bible or plan anything; the group is just for sharing.

He has also led a small group tailored for college students that has a **mission** focus. That group's purpose is to pray and brainstorm ways to reach out to a nearby college campus. Sharing is part of the equation, but they primarily spend their time praying for the campus, planning events, and evaluating how things are going.

In my youth ministry, we have Sunday evening small groups that meet for the final 45 minutes of our two-hour youth group gathering. The purpose of these groups is **sharing *and* discussion** related to the Bible lesson they've just experienced. In essence, the big-picture goal of these groups is **discipleship**. At other times in our history, we've had small groups focused on **evangelism**; our teenagers were focused on inviting friends to explore a relationship with Jesus.

For your group to be effective, it must have a clear purpose that defines how you spend your time together.

How to Decide on a Group Purpose

You probably already know why you want to lead your small group. But if you haven't yet clarified the group's purpose, consider why you were drawn to serve in the first place. You'll probably find your purpose right there!

If you need a little more help clarifying your purpose, think about these questions:

1. What do you want to be different in the world as a result of your group?

2. How do you want the members of your group to be different when the group ends?

3. What issues do you see in your teenagers that you'd like your group to address?

4. Picture your dream for the group—what would constitute a "perfect" group?

Yes, every group can have multiple purposes, but it's important to translate the purpose (or purposes) into a single sentence.

Some potential group purposes:

- To explore Jesus' heart, not just his moral teaching.

- To understand what it means to be a man or woman of God.

- To grow in intimacy with God and each other.

- To understand the youth-group teaching.

- To lead a middle school youth group.

Single Gender or Coed?

Another decision to make is whether your group is going to be same-gender or coed. There are advantages and disadvantages to both kinds. The final decision really depends on your purpose.

Our weekly discipleship groups are same-gender because we've found that our teenagers are more likely to open up about what's going on in their lives when it's all guys or all girls. But that tracks back to our purpose. If your purpose, instead, is to explore the heart of Jesus, not just his moral teachings, then a coed group might strengthen and broaden the experience. Also, mixed-gender groups work well in specific settings such as retreats, mission trips, and evangelistic or leadership groups. The advantage of coed groups is that they help kids build strong, honoring, "normal" opposite-gender relationships—they learn to see each other as brothers and sisters.

Multi-Age Groups

The choice between a same-age or multi-age group is similar to the gender question—it all depends on your overarching purpose. The multi-age dynamic layers on new challenges: The conversation in the group will need to work for both the older and younger. That means your interactive structure must "force" participation for everyone, to make sure the younger kids don't hold back because they're intimidated. For example, grouping and re-grouping kids in pairs, trios, and foursomes raises their participation level; so does going around the circle to have each person answer a question at least once. If the older students are invested and mature enough, they will naturally "help" the younger ones. And sometimes the younger ones have a lot to offer the older ones!

Every Group Has a Life Cycle

Small groups are like all living things: They're born, they grow (in size or in trust), and they eventually die. It's helpful to remember this when a group is stuck in that awkward early stage—you can't compare that experience to those iconic, mature groups you've experienced in the past. That's not fair, because every group goes through stages of growth, including...

1. *Polite Stage*—There's very little tension because people are trying not to offend one another. At this stage the relationships can feel stiff or awkward.

2. *Evaluation Stage*—Kids make decisions about how much (and whether) they will commit to the group.

3. *Family Stage*—There is trust and genuine affection for one another. This generally happens at the end of an extended period of time together.

4. *Outreach Stage*—The group has matured enough to focus outward, to minister to others outside of the group.

5. *Closure Stage*—It's very important for your group to end well. This happens naturally at the graduation transition points (8th grade and 12th grade). When the time comes, think about how to provide a context for your group to end your time together well.

How to Help Your Group Thrive

No matter the purpose of your group, we want to help you make it a great environment for growth and lifelong impact. In his book *The Road Less Traveled*, M. Scott Peck describes the romantic phenomenon of two people who fall in love. Their "ego boundaries" come down. All of us have walls protecting our hearts. When we form close relationships, we allow others past our walls, and our boundaries come down. In the same (nonromantic) way, a thriving small group offers kids an environment that's safe enough to let their boundaries come down. The two biggest levers that influence this dynamic are **time** and **trust**.

- **Time**—Yes, love at first sight is a thing, but in most romantic relationships, the couple first spends lots of time together as friends. Somewhere along the way, the magic happens. When I first met my wife, she was dating someone else and I wasn't particularly drawn to her. We had *zero* romantic interest in one another. Then her boyfriend broke up with her, and we found ourselves on a retreat where we got to know each other a lot better. I never would've fallen in love with her had we not spent extended time together.

Now, I don't want to overuse the romantic analogy in the context of a small group, but it's a real thing. In fact, as the leader, you're kind of like a matchmaker whose job is to help kids in the group grow to love each other. The easiest way to do that is to make sure they spend *extended time* together.

Technology is greatly reducing kids' face-to-face time. And research is telling us that this deprivation is creating in them a craving for more intimate, in-person relationships. That felt need is a huge win for the church. THAT'S WHAT WE DO! Even a simple weekend retreat can be a big relationship-builder. In a typical week, my teenagers spend a maximum of three hours with me at church. But a weekend retreat lasts 48 hours—that's *16 times* the normal amount of time they spend together, all in a single weekend! This extended time together (including the time trapped together in a car or van) produces shared experiences, common teaching backgrounds, and inside jokes. All of this will boost the quality and depth of your relationships.

I can't really overemphasize the value of retreats, camps, conferences, and mission trips. If your context isn't conducive for overnight events, consider alternate ways to spend longer stretches of time together as a group—for example, game nights, movie nights, serving together locally, or "field trips." After you've had a fun night together, your next small-group time will be noticeably better. Extended time together moves your group from awkward to awesome.

• **Trust**—Thriving small groups have developed a sense of trust. Hold to the "Las Vegas" rule for your group: What happens here stays here. There are exceptions, of course—if you feel a student might harm himself or others, you must alert your leaders immediately. In Chapter 4 we'll cover this in depth. It's also crucial to create an environment where kids know they won't be made fun of, even if it's "lighthearted." Trust is hard won and easily broken—and nothing is more toxic than teasing or mockery. And if kids discover that something they said in small group has been repeated outside of it, without their knowledge or permission, they may never show up again.

Once we've established a **trusting** environment, fueled by extended stretches of **time** together, now what?

Community vs. Content

Should you prioritize community-building or intentional spiritual growth in your small group? Sometimes it can feel like an either/or trade-off. Deciding which purpose to prioritize during your short time together will depend on where the group is spiritually and relationally. If you're just getting started, and especially early in the school year, community-building is an important foundation for the group. But, of course, our overarching purpose is to draw teenagers into a deeper relationship with Jesus, so how are we supposed to "make disciples" if we don't have a biblical/spiritual/Jesus focus in the group?

We know, "nobody cares how much you know until they know how much you care." This tension can lead us into an unconventional strategy: We make the pursuit of spiritual growth an interactive thing in the group. That means we're building community by asking kids to explore spiritual truths together—in pairs, trios, foursomes, or the whole group. This strategy depends on spiritually focused questions that spark real conversations. And not all questions are created equal. We need questions that challenge kids to discover truths, "thinking" questions that can't be answered "yes" or "no" or with a one-word answer or with an obvious answer. Horizontal community-building (between the teenagers) and vertical community-building (between the teenagers and Jesus) can happen simultaneously, but it will require an intentional approach that shares with kids the responsibility for discovering truth. But no matter what, it's important to take the "long" approach with your group. Let me explain...

If you're the leader of a small group for high school guys, and you're starting with freshmen, consider where you want that group to be four years from now. If you don't start off with a deep dive into biblical exploration right away, that's okay. I tell the leaders of our freshmen guys, "Your goal is to get these guys saying, 'I love being here. These guys are my friends, and I trust my leader.' " Developmentally, freshman boys are often not yet ready to *deeply* engage in biblical exploration (but there are many exceptions, of course). I know I sure wasn't. With less-mature teenagers, our goal is to focus on foundational truths and teach them that...

- the church is their home,

- the people in the church are their family,

- Jesus loves them, and

- the small group is a safe place to be.

If you're successful with these goals, teenagers will likely keep coming back through their junior and senior years, when their emerging maturity will help them grasp more complex concepts of discipleship. As you establish trust over time, you can engage your teenagers at a deeper level. We don't *over*estimate a freshman's capacity to dive in, but we also don't *under*estimate what maturing students are ready for. Here's the truth: If you raise the bar, your kids will rise to meet it. Older students (and some younger ones) already are asked to write demanding research papers, solve complex math equations, produce scripted video presentations, and figure out what "physics" is all about. This tells us they can certainly engage in a significant way with Bible exploration, experiential relationship with Jesus, and more complex theological discoveries.

What's Your Spiritual Focus?

The next question to address is, "What will you use to focus your kids' attention on Jesus and biblical/spiritual truths?" In my context, our small groups meet on the same night as our large-group gathering. Our small groups focus (in a conversational way) on the point of the large-group teaching. I create discussion questions that the groups can use if they'd like. If your purpose for small groups is different, you may have them follow a curriculum, a series of lessons, a particular Scripture focus, a video series, or even a book study. (You can find quality resources for all these options. One good place to start is group.com.)

As a general rule, you'll want to find teaching resources that help teenagers understand their place in God's story, from the Old Testament through the New Testament. Avoid lessons that focus only on changing your kids' behavior—the "tips and techniques" of the Christian life. You will want resources that focus on helping them deepen their relationship with Jesus and learn to live as his "body" in the world.

Getting Things Started

Many small groups use an icebreaker question to get the discussion started. Some resources already incorporate icebreaker questions, but you can find endless options online. Icebreaker questions typically require every teenager in the group to answer them, ensuring everyone has a voice. The best ones are easy to answer because they're focused on the person, not an idea. I mean, "What's the most fun you've ever had on a vacation?" versus "What makes a vacation fun?"

A staple in many small groups is to start with "highs and lows" for the week. This practice is also known as "roses and thorns," "stanks and danks," "happies and crappies," or my personal favorite from a group of freshman girls, "strawberries and buttholes." (Note: I didn't make that up; I couldn't make that up.) Essentially, it's a "check-in" time for kids. But there's a big downside to this common practice. I've heard from many small-group leaders that they are eliminating this kind of check-in because it ends up dominating the group's time, shoving aside time for spiritual growth. You know your group best, so you'll need to decide if "highs and lows" are worth the time they require.

Good Questions

Once you've broken the ice and kids are sharing, it's time to transition into "meatier" questions. Some "rules of thumb":

1. Ask questions that you'd want to answer. You'll know if your question meets this standard even as it's coming out of your mouth. In advance, simply ask yourself: How would I answer this? If you're confused or wrestling too much or the question seems condescending (an obvious answer or a yes-or-no answer or a cheesy answer), it's a bad question. If the question generates energy in you, it's probably a good one. But you must picture how *you* would actually answer the question; some questions look good on paper but are conversation-stoppers when you try to answer them.

In general, you want to move from factual questions (observations everyone can agree on) to more challenging questions. For example, a factual question is, "Where did Jesus take his disciples just before he was arrested?" Challenging questions often begin with "Why"—for example, "Why did that part of the passage affect you?" Do everything you can to foster an environment in which teenagers aren't afraid to speak up and aren't afraid to disagree. Encourage respectful disagreement as "normal" in your group, and invite contrasting perspectives often.

2. Ask questions that don't have obvious answers. Our goal as small-group leaders is to encourage teenagers to come to conclusions on their own, as opposed to spoon-feeding them the "right" answers. This is called "discovery learning." You and they are discovering truth together. Real discipleship won't happen without it. You want your kids to wrestle with their answers and dig for new insights. This will happen organically when they know that 1) it's a safe place to disagree, and 2) you ask open-ended questions and even play the devil's advocate to fuel the conversation. Jesus often "answered" questions by asking more questions. We can do the same. And if you're following the discussion questions in a small-group resource, synthesize them into your own words and ask them in the context of the discussion. If necessary, change the questions from conversation-killers to conversation-starters.

What does a bad question look like? Usually, they're so obvious and leading that they're embarrassing to answer. They insult our intelligence. Let's say your group is studying the Sermon on the Mount and you're focusing on the passage about loving our enemies. A bad question: "Should we show love to our enemies?" *Of course, we already know that's the standard Jesus has set.* So why ask such a no-brainer? A better question: "Why would Jesus give us such an impossibly high standard for love?" or "When have you 'loved an enemy,' and what happened as a result?" Expect more of your students, and they will rise to the occasion.

3. Ask questions that prod them to tell stories. When we ask questions that require kids to tell a story about themselves or their experiences, we give them a more accessible way to join the conversation and we help them make personal connections with each other. For example, for an icebreaker, "What's the scariest thing that ever happened to you involving an animal?" Or for something a little deeper, "When in your life has God been most real to you?" or "What's the worst trouble you've ever gotten in for disobeying your parents?"

4. Ask questions that are surprising, specific, and personal.

Let me explain...

- *Surprising* means you include something in the question that would take most people off guard. It creates interest and intrigue. For example, "What are ways we *convince* people to do something without forcing them?"

- *Specific* means you narrow the question from a broad focus to a very narrow focus. For example, "Why did Jesus essentially call the Gentile woman in Matthew 15 a 'dog'?" Your question should address only one well-defined target. So many bad questions are really two questions in one, so stick to one question per question, please.

- *Personal* means the question includes something that requires a personal response, not a theoretical response. It requires people to share out of their hearts, not just their heads. For example, "Are you typically quick to forgive or slow to forgive, and why?"

Leading a Simple Bible Study

While there are many excellent small-group Bible study resources, one of the most rewarding things to do in a group is to simply read the Bible together, then discuss and analyze it. This is a lot easier than it sounds, and it doesn't require you to be a Bible expert. Here's the secret that those of us with seminary degrees don't want you to know: The Bible speaks for itself! You don't have to have advanced training, or even believe in God, to discover truth in it. Here's a three-step process you can follow:

Step 1: Pick a Bible passage to study. For beginner studies, I usually recommend starting with one of the Gospels, although any book in the New Testament will work just fine. I like the Gospels because they are written in narrative form and spotlight the things Jesus said and did. Start at the beginning and go through it a chapter at a time or a paragraph at a time. You can start pretty much anywhere and get something out of it. Another approach is to focus on a certain character trait or practice of Jesus—his miracles or parables, for example.

Step 2: Craft your questions. The method we're suggesting is called "inductive" Bible study. (Years ago, people knew what that word actually meant. It needs a better name.) Essentially, we're seeking to learn from the Bible based *only* on what we find in the text. At the heart of inductive Bible study is asking questions about the passage in three categories:

- *Category 1 (Observation)* involves looking at the text itself. Ask questions like "How would those who first heard this passage understand this?" and "What themes emerge as you read the passage as a whole?"

- *Category 2 (Interpretation)* involves taking the information and trying to figure out what it means. Ask questions like "What is the main point the writer is trying to make?" and "What does the passage tell us about Jesus, and what does it tell us and about ourselves?"

- *Category 3 (Application)* involves understanding how the text impacts our lives and what action it requires. Ask questions like "In what ways does this passage impact your everyday life?" and "How do you feel challenged by this passage, and why?"

Step 3: Lead the Bible study. Read the passage out loud twice, and then give people time to read it by themselves once. Then go through the questions you've prepared.

In the next chapter, we'll unpack how to effectively lead your group, but I want to close with a final story to illustrate your role as a small-group leader.

Bring the Party

When I was in college, my friend Britt and I traveled to the new home of our friend Gil in Birmingham, Alabama, for New Year's Eve. We went out for dinner and stuffed ourselves with ribs. Then, of course, we stopped by Krispy Kreme and quickly consumed a dozen doughnuts. And then it was time to figure out where to ring in the New Year. I don't remember which one of us had the idea, but we decided we'd go to a grocery store, buy a bunch of party decorations (streamers, blowers, party hats), and then take them to a Waffle House for a midnight countdown. So at 11:45 we barged into a Waffle House and started asking the patrons, "Who wants a party hat?" The workers didn't skip a beat; they acted like they knew we were coming: "Oh yeah, I'll take one of those." We hung the streamers, passed out all the blowers and hats, and then led the entire restaurant in a midnight countdown. We even got free waffles (although I wasn't terribly hungry—something to do with the ribs and doughnuts). It was the most memorable New Year's Eve I've ever experienced.

So what did we do that night at the Waffle House? We *brought the party* to a group of people who had very low expectations for that night. They weren't at a cocktail party or a club; they were at a Waffle House. But this is what you have the opportunity to do each week as you lead your small group. Bring them the party—translated, that means give them your undivided attention, shepherd them through their difficult situations, and offer grace when they "miss the mark." They're expecting just another night at the Waffle House, so they'll likely be bowled over when you bring the party.

CHAPTER CODA

For this chapter's Coda, I present to you a photo from the Waffle House—
New Year's Eve, 1995.

How to Lead a Great Small Group

(by Syler)

We've already laid the groundwork for this chapter in the previous chapter. Now your kids are arriving, and it's time to get started. What key things do we need to do on "game day"?

Room Layout

Where you meet is important. Even if you can't control all aspects of your meeting environment, your room layout is still worth thinking about.

First, you want to create a space that's **comfortable**—couches are better than folding chairs. In fact, the *floor* might be better than folding chairs. If you're in a church conference room, you'll need to get creative—for example, move some sack chairs or large pillows into the room.

Second, you want a space that is **welcoming**. If you're in a room with harsh fluorescent lighting, consider bringing in a lamp or two to create a warmer vibe. If the room's chairs are in rows or around a table, create a circular layout instead. Provide food or drinks—even simple snacks help teenagers feel welcome.

Third, you want a space that is **safe**. This means meeting in a place that's private, where you can have uninterrupted time together. If you're meeting in a den where family members are coming in and out, it's unlikely teenagers will feel comfortable opening up. Consider moving to a basement or another room where you can have more privacy.

Other things to consider: It's helpful to think about the dynamics of the layout of the *people* in the group. For example, you don't want a layout that makes it hard for kids to see one another. Set things up so that the group is in a rough circle, where everyone can see everyone. When a group is new, this can be difficult. Some simply flop themselves on whatever looks comfortable. It's best to have the space set up so they're naturally drawn to sit in the circle. (We put those bird spikes on surfaces we don't want kids to sit on—they work). Make sure everyone is basically on the same level. When some are on the floor and some are on chairs (or desks or teeter-totters), it creates a physical division that has to be overcome. If you have couches, make sure you have other seating that's on the same level.

In the Beginning

If your small groups follow a large-group gathering, make sure you're not just connecting with other leaders. Sit with the teenagers, and invite connection throughout the gathering. Take advantage of the time you have walking from large group to small group by making a simple connection with a student: "Hey, I know you were worried about that test. How'd it go?" or "Have things gotten any better with that friend at school?" or "What was the best part of your week?" That one-minute conversation with a teenager really helps build a relational environment.

Now here you are, ready to launch into your small-group time. Now what?

1. Managing technology—Smartphones are everywhere, so you'll need to figure out how to handle that in your group. On the one hand, you don't want to be a cold dictator, forcing them to surrender their phones to participate. On the other hand, handheld distractions are...distracting. Begin your first gathering by asking kids for their ideas about what to do. They know that their phones can be distracting, and they'll likely have great suggestions for dealing with them. Of course, if their ideas don't really address the problem, be ready to adjust on the fly.

2. Managing cliques—Even within your small group, sub-groups can form. Before I tell you how to fight these "cliques," I'll first defend them a little. A clique is just a group of friends that someone feels excluded from. If you're in the clique, you'll likely say, "Wait, we aren't a clique. We're just friends. We're not *trying* to exclude anyone!" Most of us have been part of a clique at some point, maybe without even knowing it. You can't stop this from happening, but you can set the tone and the example by making sure everyone feels included.

First, encourage your kids to make "horseshoes, not circles." In other words, keep the strength of the closeness of your group (the U end of the horseshoe), but always leave room for others to be welcomed (the open end). In many cases, your teenagers don't even know they're functionally excluding others. If you sensitively address this dynamic from the start, you'll raise their awareness and help them correct it.

You can break down the walls cliques build by simply breaking into pairs, trios, or foursomes for portions of your discussion. Vary how you do it and your kids will have a chance to connect with everyone in the group over the course of time. If you have a persistent problem with distraction when some teenagers sit next to each other, make sure you're regularly mixing up the seating arrangement.

3. Consider crafting a covenant—One of the best ways to build unity and manage cliques is to invite the group to come up with a set of rules to live by—a group covenant. Not only are covenants valuable for building trust and maintaining accountability, but the covenant-making process itself is an incredible group-builder. Here's an example covenant that one of Steven's groups came up with:

IN THIS GROUP, WITH THE HELP OF GOD, WE WILL...

1. Strive to put Jesus and his desires before all other things.

2. Treat one another with respect and love by:

   - Not putting each other down.

   - Defending one another even when we're apart.

   - Letting each other know clearly when we're angry, resentful, or hurt—before we talk to any other person.

   - Forgiving one another when we've been hurt.

3. Spur each other to serve Jesus in the world by doing good deeds for the people around us, even when we don't like or know them.

Five Leadership Components for Leading Your Group

Once your group is up and running and you've launched into your discussion, your job now shifts to leading a thriving conversation. Some things to consider...

1. Be aware of your body language. If you're slumped in your chair and checking your phone, you're communicating that you don't care. Sit up, lean in, and keep your body language open.

2. Be an active listener. As teenagers share, active listening is very important. Nodding, smiling, and offering small words of encouragement will motivate them to keep sharing. When students stop speaking, consider using a summary statement to help them wrap up their thoughts, especially if they're having trouble "landing the plane." For example, "So it sounds like what you're saying, Sarah, is that you've really struggled with this question of how God can allow suffering. Is that right? Thanks for sharing that."

3. Vulnerability begets vulnerability. Most groups will take awhile to get comfortable with each other. Kids won't just show up and open up. But you can seed vulnerability in the group by going first. If you're willing to risk your vulnerability, you'll invite others to do the same.

4. Keep the ball in the air. The "ball of conversation" needs to stay in the air, and you're the one who can help keep it there. Read kids' body language, and encourage those who might have something to share but are holding back: "Colleen, you seem like you want to share. What are you thinking?" You can also use summary statements as a springboard to invite others to share: "Heather, I hear you saying you don't like what that Bible verse says. Does anyone else feel the same way?" You don't have to fill every moment of silence; just gently keep that ball jumping around the room.

5. Practice radical hospitality. I once stayed at a fancy-schmancy tropical resort where the staff went above and beyond to take care of their guests. I was greeted with a smile by every staffer I met. If I called the front desk from my room, the staffer answered me by name. If I asked for directions to something on the property, the staffer would walk me there instead. I felt very cared for. So think of yourself as Director of Hospitality for the fanciest-schmanciest resort ever—obviously, your small group. Go above and beyond to make your "guests" feel welcome. Henri Nouwen says, "Hospitality is not to change people, but to offer them space where change can take place." That's what you are—a space-giver to allow the Holy Spirit to work.

Some weeks you'll feel like the Glory of God hath descended from on high to bless your gathering. But other weeks you'll think you're the worst leader in the history of time. Stay calm, and above all, don't let discouragement undermine your perseverance.

Leading Groups With Specific Challenges

Some groups require lots of encouragement to share, while others need a referee. Here's how to navigate the particular challenges of your group.

- **Quiet groups**—If your group is painfully quiet, don't panic. And don't feel like it's your job to fill that quiet space with your voice. Some groups are just quieter than others, so be prepared with conversation-starters (you'll find lots of them in the Chapter Coda on page 51). Enjoy the chill vibe! Don't be afraid to ask specific teenagers to answer specific questions, and always invite them to tell stories about themselves.

- **Loud groups**—If your group is exceptionally rambunctious, again, don't panic! Energy is a good thing; you just need to learn how to harness it for good. Start by setting ground rules—for example, only one person can speak at a time! Find some object that gives kids permission to speak in the group (à la the conch shell in *Lord of the Flies*) or a word or sound you can yell that's a reminder to quiet down. Remember that in every "loud" group there are bound to be some quieter kids who are annoyed at how rowdy it is, so keep your eyes out for them and make a point of inviting their participation.

- **Awkward groups**—These look a lot like quiet groups, but there's a different species of tension in an awkward group. Opposites don't always attract, and kids who wouldn't normally group together at school sometimes need an extra push to overcome their barriers. Schedule a group outing to facilitate bonding. Make sure you're serving kid-friendly food; it's the great equalizer and will give them an excuse to interact.

Responding to Individual Challenges

Beyond group dynamics, you'll need to know how to respond to specific types of teenagers who will challenge your leadership in one way or another. For example...

- **Talkie McTalkerson**—Talkie is the guy who answers every question first and just sort of dominates your meeting. It's up to you as the leader to make sure everyone in the group has a chance to share. So in the moment, you'll need to lovingly encourage Talkie to let others speak. A simple "Do you agree or disagree with Talkie? Freddie, what do you think?" might do it. Once you've developed a stable relationship with Talkie, consider talking to him one-on-one: "I love your eagerness to share in our group! Can you help me get some of the others more involved?" The idea is to make Talkie your partner, not crush his spirit. Affirm Talkie's ability to jump in and participate, and invite him to use that gift to help others.

- **Queenie the Drama Queen**—Queenie, bless her heart, has a well-stocked pantry full of feelings. Tears come quickly for her. The whole world seems against her. Because overemotional teenagers can wear out your empathy, you'll feel an impulse to ignore Queenie. But that has the opposite effect on her. Just like every teenager in your group, Queenie needs to know it's a safe place for her to be herself. Lead the way in listening to Queenie. Practice "active listening" so she knows you understand how she feels. But then find a way to transition back to the whole group: "Queenie, that sounds really hard. I'm very glad you shared about how you're feeling. Why don't we take a moment to pray for Queenie?" Then ask one person to pray, not many. Chances are, if she's been able to share briefly and feel heard and loved, you can move on with your time together.

- **Bobby the Bump-on-a-Log** *(whose parents make him come)*—
Bobby doesn't want to be there. Maybe you know this because he flat-out
told you. He looks at his phone every 30 seconds. He rolls his eyes a
lot. He's annoyed that you exist. So the first step with Bobby is to do
everything you can to engage with him—just don't be too overt about it.
Figure out what Bobby enjoys, and ask him about it. Even grumpy people
like to talk about themselves. Slowly but surely, Bobby might decide he
doesn't absolutely hate attending the group as much as he used to. If
that fails, and if after many tries Bobby's participation in the group is a
distraction, you'll need to get his parents involved in a strategy.

- **Willa the Wallflower**—Willa loves the wall because she's allergic to
attention. Her mission is to sink into the background. She doesn't want
to be ignored, but she doesn't want to be spotlighted, either. If you're
more of an extrovert, ask an introvert in your life how he or she likes to
be treated in a group setting. You'll likely need to go out of your way to
engage with Willa, because you might forget she's there. But often, still
waters *do* run deep. If you can get her involved, you'll be surprised by
how much she contributes.

- **Danny the Distracter**—Danny means well. He's not a bad kid. He
just can't get out of his own way. It might be an ADHD issue, or it could be
related to something going on at home, but Danny causes problems in the
group. He prevents other people from engaging. If no one stops him, it will
cause real problems—others might stop coming. Your leadership here is
crucial. When possible, don't call out Danny in front of everyone; it's best
to have a private conversation with him. But if the group can't operate as
it needs to, then you must step in. Grab Danny afterward and say, "Hey,
I am so glad you're part of our group. I think you know there are times you
cause distractions, and I want to make sure others are getting everything
they can out of the group. Let's figure this out together—what can we do?"

Leave Them With a Challenge

It's important to end each session well, and in a minute we'll talk about different ways you can close with prayer. But I want to give you one final challenge: End each small-group gathering with a challenge. When it's appropriate and possible, find one takeaway from the discussion and challenge your kids to live it out before the next meeting. For example, if you've been talking about evangelism, challenge them to have a spiritual conversation with a non-believing friend that week. If you've been talking about prayer, challenge them to incorporate the prayer strategy you've been discussing into their own prayer lives. Check in during the week to remind them, and then open the following session by asking how they did. This is a no-pressure challenge; the invitation is just that—an invitation. It's not a command. (By the way, Group's popular LIVE small-group curriculum includes a unique feature called the LIVE Dailies. It's an easy way to stay in touch with your students during the week, connected to the theme of your last gathering. Go to group.com/live for more.)

Dealing With Sporadic Attendance

If some group members don't attend regularly, you'll have a hard time going deeper. Following up with teenagers when they've "gone missing" is the key. Send a simple text that says, "Hey, we missed you this week." There's a good chance that this simple effort to connect will draw them back the following week. And don't be afraid to enlist the aid of other small-group members in your follow-up efforts. "Positive peer pressure" can be a powerful encouragement.

Using Affirmation Exercises

Another option to keep in mind for your group (especially those that have gotten to know each other relatively well) is some kind of affirmation exercise. Basically, each teenager experiences positive feedback from the others. This is a powerful community-builder, and here are two ways to do it.

1. **The Affirmation Circle**—One person sits in the center of the group, and the other teenagers say something positive about that person. Even though it can be hard to sit still and receive affirmation from others, the praise sinks in. It both raises the confidence of your kids and bonds them more closely to each other.

2. **The Compliment Card**—If kids in your group have a hard time expressing themselves verbally, have them write their affirmations instead. Give each young person a piece of paper with his or her name at the top. Then have kids each pass their papers to the person next to them. They take a moment to write something true and good about the person whose name is at the top of the sheet, then pass it on to the next person. This continues until each teenager gets his or her own paper back. I've known students who've kept this sheet of paper for years after their group ended.

Now, what sort of "prompts" can you give kids for either the Affirmation Circle or Compliment Card exercises?

1. What you most appreciate about this person.

2. One way you've seen Jesus move through this person.

3. One gift or talent you see in this person.

4. A blessing you'd like to give to this person.

5. One thing you like about what this person is wearing (helpful for a new person who doesn't know anyone).

TWO GROUND RULES FOR AFFIRMATION EXERCISES:

1. Nothing negative, even if it's meant as a joke (this is hard, because kids use jokes to diffuse tension).

2. The person receiving the affirmation is not allowed to discount it.

Use Journals to Open Up Participation

If your group has a hard time focusing, use journaling as a way to capture their attention. Buy a simple journal for each teenager, or just make them yourself using a computer template. Begin your time by asking them to journal their response to a reflective question, based on your lesson material. When you force kids to be quiet at the beginning of your time, you have a better chance of opening up sharing for everyone later on, especially for the quieter students. When you know everyone has journaled a response, you can ask the quiet ones to share what they've written. Because they tend to be introverts, they're much more thoughtful in their writing. Last, encourage your teenagers to leave the journals with you or they'll never remember to bring them back. Promise, of course, that you won't read them.

Creative Ways to Close in Prayer

Communal prayer will help your kids connect both to Jesus and to each other. Our purpose is to guide them into a deeper relationship with Jesus and form them into a community that the Holy Spirit can live inside. Communal prayer is crucial in this process. Here's a menu of possibilities:

1. Have each young person share a prayer request while the group writes down each request. Then kids agree to pray for one another during the week. If you have the time, ask a dependable member of the group to briefly pray for each request. If time is an issue, you can pray for the needs yourself and make sure you do it in a timely way.

2. Have each teenager pray for the person to his or her right or left.

3. Break into pairs or trios to share prayer requests, and then have them pray for each other. Encourage these smaller groups to follow up later in the week via text.

4. If you see cliques developing, you may want to *assign* prayer partners so kids get to know each other better.

5. In more mature groups, experiment with some form of "listening prayer." Put one teenager in the center of the group, then give everyone a minute of silence to listen to Jesus on behalf of that person before they pray. Tell them to simply ask, "Jesus, how would you like me to pray for _____ ?" After the minute of silence, invite all those who received a "nudge" from the Spirit to pray for the person in the center.

CHAPTER CODA

For this chapter's Coda, I present to you, courtesy of one of my leaders (thanks, Joanna!) a list of 20 conversation-starter questions. Enjoy!

1. One-Word Check-In: Go around the circle and have each person give one word to describe how he or she feels in that moment. Give kids a little time to think before sharing.

2. Spiritual Prayer Requests: Ask for prayer requests but only for *spiritual needs.*

3. Can you explain the passage/verse/concept briefly, in your own words?

4. Why did God think it was necessary to include this passage/verse in the Bible?

5. Who in your life has modeled this passage/verse/concept?

6. In what ways have you worshipped Jesus recently?

7. How have you experienced the presence of Jesus this week?

8. What has Jesus been teaching you lately?

9. What word best expresses how you feel about Jesus right now?

10. Describe a time in your life you felt most loved/appreciated/hopeful/joyful (and so on).

11. How are you pursuing Jesus in your life right now?

12. What habits do you practice in your prayer life/thought life/Scripture-study life?

13. How are your friends/family/environment affecting you positively and negatively?

14. What have you been struggling with lately?

15. What do you need to start doing and stop doing right now?

16. How have you felt the Holy Spirit influencing your life?

17. What does conviction feel like to you? How do you know when Jesus is convicting you of something?

18. How can we, as a group, help you?

19. How have you seen Jesus respond to your prayers recently?

20. If you could change anything about the world instantly, what would it be, and why?

How to Help Hurting Teenagers

(by Steven)

We've covered how to plan and lead a great small group, and now it's time to turn our attention to other issues that come up when we're working with teenagers. In the next two chapters, we'll explore how to handle the hard situations that our kids are facing.

I was the new youth minister, observing my first youth group meeting. I introduced myself, then hung back to watch how the teenagers interacted with each other. At the end, a 14-year-old girl asked if she could talk to me. We retreated from the throng to a more private side of the youth room and sat down together. She said, "My name is Blanca, and since you're our new youth leader, I thought I should let you know that I have a little issue with suicide."

Hey! Welcome to working with teenagers! At least she told me her name first...

I wish this was a rare and surprising story. It's not. It's amazing how often teenagers will confess deep and troubling things to the adults in their lives. Sometimes it's a test. And sometimes it's a last-ditch effort to find an adult who cares enough to take them seriously. But small-group leaders must learn to handle tough issues with kids.

Adolescents have fully capable adult bodies (adult-size, adult-strong, adult-sexual) and many adult freedoms (spendable cash, access to transportation, a pocket supercomputer that connects them to the

WHOLE WORLD), but their experience base is closer to a child's. They confront "adult" problems but lack adult experience and support systems. So it's not surprising that they struggle, especially when you consider how much *adults* struggle with similar problems! To make things more difficult, adolescents will often hide these struggles from the people who are most invested in helping them: their parents.

On average, a teenager will go through a major crisis about once every four years. That means that if there are six kids in your small group, you'll deal with one or two crises a year. Most adolescent crises fall into one of five categories:

1) Anxiety and depression (including suicide)

2) Death of a loved one

3) Divorce

4) Drugs and alcohol

5) Sex (including romance, rape, pregnancy, molestation, as well as confusion about orientation and gender)

In this chapter, we'll cover the basics of helping teenagers through their crises. In the next chapter, we'll look at specific ways to intervene in these five crisis categories.

What *Not* to Do

What constitutes help for a teenager who's struggling? This is actually an easy question to get wrong. Adults find lots of ways to mess up "helping." So before we focus on how we can help, let's spotlight all the things we do that are *not* helpful.

- **It's not helpful to lecture.** Most of the time, teenagers who are facing a crisis already know the "right answer." By high school, they've heard a thousand lectures from their parents and teachers and school administrators and coaches about the "right answers."

In most cases, what they need are ways to live out the answers they already know. Lecturing doesn't help. Listening, reflecting, and asking questions does help.

- **It's not helpful to solve the problem for them or to tell them how we solved it when it happened to us.** When a teenager comes to us with a problem, it's his or her problem, not ours. We're not helping kids mature when we step in and fix their problems for them. Honestly, sometimes my attempts to fix a student's problem have actually made things worse. It can be reassuring for them to hear that we've had similar problems, but it's seldom helpful to go into detail about our experience.

What to Do

When a teenager comes to us with a problem, we can offer three possible responses:

1) Listen.
2) Provide applicable information or advice.
3) Refer to someone more capable.

Let's dive into each of these responses in more detail...

1. Listen.

For the majority of their problems, students just need someone to listen. They can usually figure out the right thing to do if they think about it long enough, and our listening helps them clarify and evaluate their thoughts. Listening also helps them figure out who they are. Early in life, children learn to value themselves based on how their parents value them. This is why psychotherapists focus on the relationship between the patient and his or her parents. As children enter adolescence, they shift their attention to peers and non-parental mentors like you. Our response to their problems helps them understand their value to both us and God. Let's explore how we can listen in ways that help them.

- **Listening well means treating their problems as important.** When teenagers come to us with a problem, they study our reaction to gauge if the problem is really a big deal. For example, when I was young and I got hurt, I'd cry (well into my 30s ☺). My parents (and later my children) often said things like "Stop crying" and "Stop acting like a baby; you're not hurt." So when I went to an adult with a problem, I often approached the person apologetically: "This isn't really a big deal, but I feel depressed." I watched the reaction to see if I was "being a baby."

So when teenagers come to us with *any* problem, it's important to take them seriously. We gauge the seriousness of the problem not on its surface characteristics but on how much pain it's causing them. Pain hurts. And it's their pain—and the accompanying fear, anger, guilt, and shame—that can lead to a destructive response. Pain translates to "serious."

Of course, teenagers often approach us when we're busy or distracted. When we try to multitask by listening to a teenager's problem while simultaneously attending to other priorities, we implicitly denigrate their concern. Fortunately, most teenage catastrophes don't require a first responder. By the time they get to us, the problem has usually been brewing for a while, and waiting an hour or a day to focus on it will not hurt the student or our relationship. So listening well means we clear time to focus on their problem without distractions. If I can't stop what I'm doing to give them my full attention, I'll say, "You are important to me, and I have to get this done, so let's meet later when I can focus fully on you."

When you meet with teenagers (remember, always in a public or visible place), take out your cellphone, pointedly switch it to "do not disturb" mode, then put it away. This is a sacramental action, an outward and visible sign of your inner commitment to honor the stories of your students.

- **Listening well means not talking.** The first challenge to listening well is simply to resist the urge to talk more than is needed! As soon as I think I understand a teenager's problem, I'm tempted to interrupt and offer an answer. That's more efficient, right? Well, no—for several reasons...

   1) They likely already know the right answer. They need my help processing the situation more than they need my problem-solving answers.

   2) Most young people won't tell you the real problem first. Here's a quick example: My friend Vinnie (I know...but it's actually his name) gave a talk to a high school campus Christian club. As he was leaving, one obviously upset young woman remained. He asked her what was wrong, and she told him she was mad at herself because she hadn't finished her homework. In that situation, I likely would've "solved her problem" by suggesting that she not do anything after school until her homework was finished. *"Wow, what great advice,"* she'd say to me (in my dreams). It's a good thing Vinnie is wiser than I am. He asked the girl what kept her from completing her homework. She explained that she'd planned on doing it early that morning but had slept through her alarm (another problem I could've solved for her). Vinnie kept pursuing, and she explained why she hadn't slept the night before: The noise of her drunk father beating up her mother was hard to sleep through (a problem that, finally, would've shut me up). Most teenagers don't offer up embarrassing situations easily. We have to listen, reflect, and ask follow-up questions to uncover the real problem.

- **Listening well means reflecting.** To listen with our full attention, we must reflect what we see and hear in a way that's helpful. My friend Scott Pelking, a clinical adolescent counselor, teaches reflective listening as a way to ensure kids know we're paying attention to them. Reflective listening means "noticing what we notice," then speaking it out: "You seem pretty happy right now. Did something good happen?" or "You look really sad. Can you share what's going on?" or "You sound really worn out. Are you tired?" Our active reflections invite kids to talk more, especially when they're tied to a focused question. They will respond better to "Sounds like you were surprised at his reaction; want to talk about it?" than to "Why did you say that to him?" Reflection also rivets our attention on the teenager, which they decode as care.

- **Listening well means asking questions.** To really understand what a teenager is trying to share, we have to ask clarifying questions. Often when students are troubled about something, they've turned it over in their heads so often that their description of the problem comes sputtering out of them, full of shorthand references and head-scratching assumptions. My impulse is to nod and act like I understand even when they're making no sense at all, because I want to communicate my support. But it's actually much more helpful to them, and to us, to take the time to ask clarifying questions so we really understand what the issue is. Our questions help them think!

The WDEP strategy for asking clarifying questions, developed by Robert Wubbolding, can be very helpful:

W: What do you WANT, and how badly do you want it?

D: What DIRECTION are you pursuing right now to get what you want?

E: EVALUATION—Is what you're doing actually helping you get what you want, or is it hindering you from getting it? *(This is the most important part of the strategy.)*

P: What's your PLAN if things aren't working *or* if things are working and you want to maintain what you achieved or want to improve?

Some questions are more helpful than others. For example, "why" questions that seem confrontive, judgmental, or skeptical will put students on the defensive. A confrontational approach to question-asking produces excuses ("She made me do it!" or "He hit me first!") or non-answers ("I dunno"). We never ask these kinds of "why" questions when someone has done something right! Think about it: "Why are you dressed so nicely this morning?" "Why did you do such a wonderful job on the presentation?" It's almost impossible to answer these questions, because we reserve confrontational "why" questions for people who've done something wrong.

2. Provide applicable information or advice.

With some teenage problems, we really do have input that is new and helpful to them. We may know something about the adult world or their school system or their legal rights that they've never considered. In these rare situations, it's crucial that we give them the information or advice we know. If our advice seems valuable, we need to offer it *after* listening well, offering our attentive reflections, and asking clarifying questions.

3. Refer to someone more capable.

Sometimes kids have issues that are best handled by someone who is better equipped to help. It could be another person on our ministry team or maybe a counselor, social worker, or law enforcement professional.

How do you know when to refer?

1. *When we're uncomfortable with the situation.* Maybe we lack experience in a specific area, the issue makes us uncomfortable, or we're somehow personally affected by the circumstance. I once had a 12-year-old want to talk to me about the changes her body was going through in puberty. I asked one of our female leaders to spend some time with her. This was a two-fer; I had no experience *and* it made me uncomfortable.

2. *When the problem is getting worse.* If the issue starts affecting a teenager's daily functioning, grades, health, or relationships—or it's potentially a dangerous situation—then it's important to get the student's parents involved and seek professional help.

3. *When your ministry leader determines the problem needs more help than you can give it.* Remember, if you're working on a difficult issue with one of your teenagers, you need to make sure your ministry leader knows about it.

4. *When we are legally mandated to report the problem.* We are legally mandated to inform law enforcement authorities or medical professionals when a student is...
   a) being hurt,
   b) hurting himself or herself, or
   c) planning on hurting someone else.

Most states have a child-abuse hotline. If you discover that a child is being hurt or abused by an adult in any way, that hotline is your best tool. Tell your ministry leader; perhaps the two of you can make the call together. Even though that call may remove the situation from your control, you must continue to walk with your teenager in the journey ahead.

How do you refer compassionately?

When it's time to pass a problem on to someone who is better qualified to handle it, do it compassionately. Telling teenagers they need to talk to someone else can sound like an attempt to get rid of them. Make sure the person you send them to is willing to help. Personally take the student to that person, and then check with the teenager afterward to make sure things went well. Continue to follow up as long as it seems helpful.

How do you respect confidentiality?

In general, we must hold the things our kids tell us in confidence. *However*, we must never tell teenagers that we will keep their secrets in all circumstances. Why?

First, we are not in ministry by ourselves. We're part of a team that includes our ministry leader and/or pastor (or the leader of our para-church ministry). Our team leader needs to know if something serious is going on with one of our teenagers. And they're often in a position to know things we don't know about the family involved.

Second, some problems are far beyond our ability to help. As a youth pastor, I don't want my small-group leaders to get burned out trying to help a teenager with a problem they can't handle—for example, "My father the church elder is abusing my little brother."

Third, if minors in your group are a) being hurt by an adult, b) hurting themselves, or c) planning on hurting someone, we are legally mandated to report the situation to the authorities.

Dr. Marv Penner, executive director of All About Youth in Canada and founder of The Coalition for Youth Ministry Excellence is the leading expert on counseling teenagers in youth ministry. He has developed a "Three A's" response to teenagers who share "secrets" that honors our need to report or refer but extends the conversation instead of killing it.

- **Acknowledge** that the issue is important.
- **Affirm** the courage the teenager has shown by bringing the problem to you.
- **Assure** them that from this point forward, nothing will be done behind their back or without their knowledge.

Penner says that once we've determined that the problem requires us to report or refer, we can give the teenager three options for how that can happen:

1. I can report what you've told me to the people who need to know (child protection, police, parents, and so on), and I'll get in touch with you as soon as I've done that to let you know how things went.

2. You can tell the people who need to know, but it needs to happen within the next X number of hours, and I will check in with you to make sure you've done that.

3. We can do this together, and I'll be there to support you and make sure everything is being done to take care of you during this difficult time.

On the other side of this confidentiality tension is the need to protect privacy. A student's secret is his or hers to share, not ours. So be careful not to gossip or talk to anyone not in your "chain of command" about a teenager's issue. And never, ever mention anything about the problem to another teenager.

Many times I've had a teenager start a conversation with "If I tell you something, can you promise not to tell anyone?" I've never had one walk away when I explain that while I'll take what they tell me very seriously, I can't promise to never tell.

The "Little Issue" With Suicide

I started this chapter with the story of Blanca's "little issue with suicide." Here's the rest of that story: After listening to uncover some details, I asked her the PLAN questions (we'll focus on this strategy in the next chapter) to assess how serious the risk was. I judged the risk to be low, so I told her she needed to tell her parents. She absolutely refused. When I asked why, she told me she didn't mind her parents *knowing* about her struggle, but she just didn't want to talk to them about it. So we agreed that she'd write them a note, with a line that directed them to call me if they had questions. Sure enough, I got a call from Blanca's mother about 10:00 that night. This story has a happy ending. Blanca's older sister had dealt with similar issues, so after our late-night conversation, Blanca's parents made an appointment with a good counselor. Over the months that followed, they worked through her depression together.

I've often told this story when I train interns and volunteers, and last year one of the interns told me she knew who "Blanca" was. She'd just been to our church's women's retreat, and Blanca, now married and on our church worship team, was one of the presenters. She told her story at the retreat. So, yes, our work with teenagers really matters; we are an extension of Jesus (his body), a conduit for blessing in our kids' lives.

CHAPTER CODA

> A quote from our friend—the source for much of what we've stolen for this chapter:
>
> "Our job is not to solve their problems. These are their problems. Not ours.
>
> Our job is not to make kids feel better. God allows pain.
>
> Our job is not to make them happy. Our job is to help them become successful, Christian adults."
>
> —Dr. Dana Max

How to Handle Tough Situations

(by Steven)

One of the reasons I didn't panic when Blanca told me she wanted to kill herself was that I've had this kind of conversation before. We've both had lots of conversations with teenagers about troubling things.

In this chapter, we'll share our hard-earned wisdom about how to respond in these situations. As you're reading, keep in mind what we've already said about listening, reflecting, and asking clarifying questions.

Anxiety, Depression, and Suicide

Anxiety and depression are growing problems among teenagers. Some sociologists say this is related to their increased use of social media and the deceptive isolation it encourages, but many other factors are contributors. There are two types of anxiety and depression that we need to spotlight. The first type might be called *situational*—in other words, it's related to something that has recently happened such as a romantic breakup, a school problem, or a family issue. The second type is *long-term or ongoing* anxiety or depression. Either type can lead to clinical depression. Here's a simple way to assess whether or not a teenager is clinically depressed.

First, ask if the teenager is currently under treatment for depression. If not, ask if he or she has ever been diagnosed with depression. A student who has had issues in the past is likelier to need help from a trained counselor.

Second, check with the teenager to see if he or she is experiencing any of these issues:

◊ Has the student experienced a significant loss recently?

◊ Over the past two weeks has the student felt:

» more irritable that usual?
» more tearful than usual (cries at almost anything)?
» helpless?
» hopeless?
» worthless?

◊ Over the past two weeks, has the student experienced changes in energy, sleeping, eating or had "passive death wishes"—for example, "If I didn't wake up this morning, I wouldn't care"?

If the teenager answers yes to four or more of the questions above and/or indicates changes in energy (less), sleeping (more or less), and eating (more or less), then there's a high probability he or she is dealing with major depression and needs to see a professional. Obviously, that requires the involvement of parents and your ministry leader. (Refer to Marv Penner's "Three A's" on page 62.) Your ministry leader will have connections to Christian counselors in the area and can make recommendations to the parents.

We recently had one of our 12-year-olds, a vivacious and usually cheery girl, tell her small-group leader on a retreat that she was tired of smiling all the time. The leader took her aside to ask what she meant. The girl told her that she felt like she had to keep up her smile for the people around her but that she was almost always sad inside. The leader assessed ongoing depression, and not connected to anything that had recently happened, so we went to the parents and they arranged for her to start meeting with a Christian counselor.

    1. Assessing suicide risk. Suicide is now the second-leading killer of teenagers and quickly gaining on the top cause, "unintentional injury." The path to suicide is prompted by situational or ongoing depression, anger, or the desire to end perceived pain. How do we handle this issue when we see the signs of it in a young person? Here's my general advice, along with a simple system for assessing suicide risk. To begin, three big-picture imperatives:

- **Don't be afraid to bring up suicide in a conversation.** I can guarantee that if you're wondering about it, they've likely already thought about it. Don't worry that if you bring this up, you'll be planting an idea they've never considered. In fact, mentioning it could be a relief to them.

- **Most (but *not* all) talk about suicide is a plea for attention.** That doesn't mean we respond complacently. If a teenager is thinking about it, the issue is serious. It doesn't matter if the situation that's upsetting them doesn't seem like a big deal to us. If they bring it up, they want your help.

- **If a teenager is contemplating suicide, we have a legal responsibility to report it.** Our job is to figure out how serious the risk is. Our friend Dr. Dana Max, a licensed clinical psychologist and former youth minister, teaches a five-question strategy for assessing suicide risk using the acrostic PLAN. I've frequently used PLAN when I deal with students considering suicide, just as I did when I talked to Blanca. The first question is simple: "Do you have a plan?"

Often teenagers will think about suicide in an abstract way. If they answer this question with a "no," the risk is lower. If they answer this question with a "yes," the risk is higher. So we follow up by asking them to describe their plan. After that, our follow-up questions each start with a letter in the word PLAN:

THE PLAN ASSESSMENT STRATEGY

Previous attempts—We ask, "Have you ever tried to commit suicide before?" If the answer is yes, then the risk skyrockets. A student who has attempted suicide before is far likelier to try it again.

Lethality of the plan—Some plans are well-developed and scary; others are unrealistic. One middle school student told me her plan was "salt and ice" and pointed to her wrist. "It'll burn right through," she said. A bad plan is not a prod for you to explain to the teenager that her plan won't work; a bad plan indicates lower risk. A well-thought-out plan means the risk is much higher. A student who answers, "I plan to go up on the roof of my house and shoot myself with a gun" has considered exactly *how, when, and where* they'll do it.

Availability—Do they have the means they need to kill themselves readily available? A teenager who plans to go up on the roof of the house still needs access to a gun. So the question we ask is, "Do you have a gun?" If they do not have a readily available way to carry out their plan, the risk is lower. If they answer, "I was thinking I would buy one at a gun show," you know the attempt isn't imminent. On the other hand, "My dad keeps a loaded pistol beside his bed" should set off our alarm bells. If they have the means and they have a specific plan, the risk is extremely high.

Network—The final question targets a longer-term priority. If you're comfortable that the risk of suicide is low, it's important to monitor the teenager's network of friends and family. Before adolescents commit suicide, they often withdraw from that network. They'll try to tie up loose ends and/or find some way to say goodbye to the people who matter to them. If a teenager suddenly stops coming to your small group, that may signal social withdrawal. Or if that teenager starts giving away important items, that's a glaring red flag. You can check their social media posts for signs as well. Finally, a paradoxical sign to watch for is a recently sad or depressed teenager who is suddenly happy. This could indicate relief because they've finally made a decision to end their life.

2. What to do if you've determined there's a risk—of suicide. A teenager with no plan or an unworkable plan might not be high-risk, but in all cases we must report what we've learned to our ministry leaders (and ideally a trained professional), who can make a more complete assessment. I give the volunteers in our youth group the phone number of an adolescent counselor who attends our church. If suicide comes up in a conversation, they know to call me and then call the counselor.

Even a low risk of suicide needs to be reported to parents. I told the "salt and ice" student that her parents needed to know and that if she hadn't told them within 24 hours, I'd tell them myself. I've never had a teenager who's struggling with depression or suicide who wanted to tell their parents. But when we explore the options, we can always figure out an acceptable way to let the parents know. The written note that Blanca wrote her parents is one example. Another student actually made an audio recording explaining what was going on with him, then asked his parents to listen to it.

Teenagers who have an elevated risk of suicide (medium risk) may have a well-developed plan but no access to the means. Kids in this stage need close monitoring. In addition to reporting the risk to a ministry leader and counseling professional, I tell my volunteers to check in with medium-risk teenagers at least once a day. Find out how they're doing, and look for signs that things are getting worse. We ask these teenagers to sign a "suicide contract" with their small-group leader that basically says, "If I decide to end my life, I promise I'll let you know first." This gives these kids an additional lifeline by introducing accountability into the relationship and accounts for any "loose ends" in your intervention strategy.

If you've assessed that a teenager is at high risk for suicide, then law enforcement authorities need to know, the parents need to know, and your ministry leader needs to know. Do your best to stay with the teenager until the authorities or the parents arrive. At this point, a professional needs to make an assessment, and that may result in the teenager being admitted to a hospital or mental health program.

If in doubt, always err on the side of safety by consulting with your ministry leader.

Death

Death happens, and we hate it. In the hope of our "new birth," we look forward to the time death is finally banished. In the meantime, it's one of the most difficult things our kids will ever experience. It often causes them to question their faith. A death that impacts our teenagers reiterates a simple reality: We can't fix their problems. And there are no "silver bullet" words that will make it all better. But that doesn't mean we are helpless in the face of death. Here's how we can help.

1. **Simply be present.** As much as your schedule and commitments allow, make yourself available, especially soon after the death.

2. **Help kids understand the death in the context of their faith** *(without lecturing).* Jesus promises us life after death. Whether or not the loved one was a believer, he or she is now entrusted to his mercy and justice. Jesus is trustworthy and loves the deceased more than anyone on earth ever could. This is not the time to talk about their loved one's "final resting place." Be humble: "I don't understand it either. All I can tell you is that Jesus is good. You may not believe that right now, but Jesus believes in you, and so do I." Be patient with the response you get back; trauma often finds a "sideways" expression in anger.

3. **Help them grieve.** The natural human reaction to loss is grief, and grieving is a process. The bigger the loss, the deeper and longer-lasting the grief. Grief washes over us in waves—at first frequent and intense, then slowly modulating over time. The five stages of grief fuel those waves (but not necessarily in a linear way).

THE FIVE STAGES OF GRIEF

- **Denial**—The shock of death can shut down the mind or prompt "magical" rationalizations ("Maybe they mistook her for someone else").

- **Bargaining**—Out of desperation, we try to make a deal with God ("If you'll just fix this, I'll go to church for the rest of my life").

- **Anger**—This misdirection of grief can happen at any time, and the target could be anybody, including Jesus, you, or the person who died.

- **Depression**—Death can shove a person into a darkness so deep that suicidal thoughts surface.

- **Resolution**—When grieving people are ready to accept the loss and move forward, they have integrated (or resolved) the death into their "new normal." This can take years.

You can help teenagers grieve by giving them a safe space to talk about what they've lost. Ask them how they're doing and specifically how they're dealing with the death. As time goes on, ask them about the person they lost—the last time they saw the person, favorite memories, or first memories. Ask to see meaningful photos when the time is right.

Hospitalization

Visit your teenagers when they are admitted to a hospital. Don't be afraid to present yourself to hospital staff as the student's "minister." You are their small-group pastor. Most hospitals allow ministers access to patient's rooms. Hospital visits should be brief, maybe 15 minutes at the top end, and make sure you pray with or for them before you leave. I usually call ahead to ask if they need anything. If there are no diet restrictions, I'll go by a coffee shop or Chick-fil-A on the way.

If you have teenagers whose family members are in the hospital, go to support them. Your church's pastoral staffers will spend time with the adults, but you can focus on supporting the students.

Divorce

A teenager's response to divorce is a lot like the grieving pattern of a death. That's because it *is* a death; a relationship that was once alive is now gone, and the feelings of loss are intense. All the guidance we've offered in the "Death" section applies. The big difference is that dead people don't have visitation schedules or run into you at Walmart. And unlike a death, divorce unfolds over an extended period of time, so our help must extend over the long haul. In a divorce there are several crisis points:

- The initial awareness that parents are splitting.
- The day one parent moves out.
- The day decisions are made about visiting rights.
- The day the divorce is finalized.

Younger students (especially) are likely to feel guilt for somehow causing the divorce. If you hear or sense this, gently reflect back the truth. Realize that teenagers with divorced parents will likely have to adjust their whole schedule to abide by a new visitation schedule. Moving back and forth between homes is tremendously difficult for them. This earthquake in their lives may take them away from friends and, often, your small group. Continue to care for these kids even when they're spending every other week away. They need someone they can safely vent to about their frustrations and grief.

Drugs and Alcohol

Drug and alcohol abuse is endemic in youth culture. Our teenagers, even the home-schooled ones, will all come into contact with others who are using drugs and alcohol. For some, casual drug use is a present reality in their friend group. They may fight you on the morality of drug and alcohol use, but alcohol, vaping, and most drugs are illegal. Getting caught with them can cause major legal headaches. And getting drunk or high *is* forbidden in Scripture (Ephesians 5:18). It's a habit that requires lying and hiding things from their parents. Jesus "came to set captives free." Drug and alcohol abuse represents an insidious form of captivity. So our role is to dig deeper into their motivations and help them move toward the better life of freedom Jesus has for them.

For a fraction of our kids, using drugs and alcohol will lead to addiction. Addiction is a disease that is progressive and terminal. The endgame is 1) death, 2) incarceration/institutionalization, and 3) ongoing recovery. Genetic factors make some teenagers more susceptible to addiction. Students with an alcoholic or addicted parent have a three-in-four chance of becoming addicted themselves. If the drug/alcohol use is habitual or the student shows up at meetings under the influence, he or she needs the help of a professional counselor.

WHEN DO YOU TELL THE PARENTS?

Now for the big question: When you discover a teenager is using drugs or alcohol, when, how, and who do you tell?

- **Always tell your ministry leader.** For the reasons we've mentioned previously, your leader always needs to know. If you think addiction might be involved, the student's parents absolutely need to know; they are the gatekeepers for getting professional help.

- **If addiction is not involved, the situation is not as clear.** Telling parents about drug/alcohol use could seem like a violation of trust by the teenager and lead to the end of your relationship. When my children were teenagers, I prayed for intelligent, godly adults who could be there for my kids when they made stupid mistakes that they felt embarrassed to tell me about. I didn't want their small-group leaders to break that confidence unless the situation was really serious.

- **Two case scenarios can help you decide what to do:**

  1) A senior higher on our leadership team went to a concert with friends who brought water bottles full of alcohol. She got drunk. She told us about it, and we told her that as a leader, the younger kids who look up to her could see her behavior as a compelling model for their own. We strongly encouraged her to tell her parents. We believed this incident was a one-time thing and she'd be better off if we didn't violate her trust by telling her parents.

  2) One of our small-group leaders met regularly with a teenager who started using drugs. The leader told her ministry leader, and they prayed about whether or not to tell the girl's parents. Then the young woman began having indiscriminent sexual relationships with guys who were using drugs with her. At this point she'd clearly put herself in danger, so the small-group leader went to the parents. They refused to believe her, and the girl felt her trust was violated, so she broke off the relationship. There is no happy ending to this story, but we made the right decision in this situation.

Sexuality

Sexual experimentation and pornography have always been huge temptations for teeangers. Though Gen Z teenagers are less likely to have sex than previous generations, it's still a big problem. When teenagers come to you with an issue related to their sexuality, it's important to express your care for them and your desire to help them make wise decisions. This advice applies to all four of the most frequent challenges kids face in this arena: sexual relationships, pornography, same-sex attraction, and gender dysphoria.

1. Sexual relationships—When kids who've grown up in the church get involved in sexual relationships, they already know what they're doing is morally wrong. So, knowing that, why did they get themselves into this situation? Our questions need to be nuanced—for example, "What would you say to yourself if you were me right now?" Any misunderstandings about biblical teaching need to be corrected at this point. Of course, it's important to make sure they know that Jesus forgives when we repent, that you'll continue to care about them no matter what, and that continuing in sexual activity will ultimately hurt them.

For teenagers who haven't grown up in the church, it may come as a shock to discover that the Bible forbids sexual activity outside of marriage. Invite them to explore with you what the Bible says about sex. Emphasize that the purpose of God's restrictions on sexual activity are an expression of his goodness and his desire for blessing in our lives. We discover true joy when we abide by the boundaries our Good Father has set out for us: "The Lord will withhold no good thing from those who do what is right" (Psalm 84:11). The greatest gift we can receive in life is Jesus himself.

So how far is too far? Many kids understand they shouldn't be sexually active in their dating relationships. But they want to know what, short of intercourse, is "acceptable" in a Christian dating relationship. In other words, *How far can I go before it's considered a sin?* It's important to challenge the assumption behind that question. When they ask "How far is too far?" they're not asking "How can I honor Jesus and this person in the relationship?" As Jesus-followers, our focus is not about what we can take but what we can give. In 1 Corinthians 6:12-20, Paul reminds us that we're to honor God with our bodies.

Help them understand that what they're doing is essentially stealing intimacy from their partner's future spouse. Later they will certainly wish they had saved that intimacy for the future. We know that few people actually marry their high school girlfriend or boyfriend. So encourage them to live the golden rule relative to their dating life: *Do unto their future spouse as you would have them do unto your future spouse.* Ask if they'd want the person they'll eventually marry to do what they're considering. Challenge them to imagine what it would be like to attend their partner's future wedding and feel good about how they honored God's relational boundaries.

If you're forced to answer the question, the only physical activity they likely won't regret is kissing. And even kissing is a "gateway drug" to more intense sexual activity. They're better off saving it for marriage and focusing on the friendship instead. Ask if they're willing to let you hold them accountable in their relationship, emphasizing what an honor it would be for you.

2. Pornography—So many guys and girls in our culture have been exposed or addicted to pornography, often before the age of 10. The initial exposure can happen in myriad ways: a "phishing" email, characters in a video game, or on social media.

At one time parents had some control over their kids' exposure to pornography, but no longer. It's almost impossible to use the internet without running into it. It's such a widespread problem that it's almost certain you have someone on your ministry team who has experienced this struggle firsthand and can offer help. Again, it's important that kids know what Jesus has to say about lust: "Anyone who even looks at [someone] with lust has already committed adultery with [them] in his heart" (Matthew 5:28). They also need to understand the heartbreaking exploitation of women and children in the porn industry and the way continued interaction with pornography can damage a person's ability to have a healthy sexual relationship in marriage.

It's important to connect kids to someone who can function as an accountability partner—someone they can confess their failures to and who can provide common-sense advice (don't take your phone, tablet, or laptop into your room alone, for example). Point them to helpful online resources and apps, including Covenanteyes.com and XXXChurch.com.

3. Same-sex attraction—There are few topics in youth ministry more controversial and difficult to tackle than same-sex attraction. Entire denominations have split over this issue. And while our earlier discussion of sexual sin focused on behavior, homosexuality extends far beyond behavior. Depending on the context you're ministering in (not to mention your own personal convictions), you may or may not agree with our perspective. Always seek to minister under the authority of your church's leaders; what we advise may or may not line up with that.

Our conviction is that the Bible makes clear that God's design for sexual activity is reserved for a man and a woman in the covenant of marriage. We won't take the time to unpack that, but we'd like to talk about how to express this understanding in the two contexts you are likeliest to encounter them: with a group of students who are asking about what the Bible says about homosexuality, and with an individual student who's experiencing same-sex attraction.

While you may not have teenagers in your group who are wrestling with same-sex attraction, you'll most certainly have kids who have gay friends. In contemporary culture, the chief "unforgivable sin" is to not show acceptance to those on the fringe, especially sexual minorities. Teaching about the Bible's design for human sexuality will sound like judgmentalism and exclusion to them. You're also more and more likely to encounter teenagers who have one or more gay parents. How can we communicate the extravagant love that God has for each person while also communicating his good design for sexuality when it appears restrictive and unfair? You'll need extended time to address this with your students. Be prepared for plenty of questions.

Here are four truths that will help as you navigate this same-sex attraction challenge:

- **Our true identity comes from Jesus, not sexuality.** Our culture tries to convince us that our primary identity is rooted in who we're attracted to sexually. That's not the teaching of the Bible. The Bible insists that our primary identity comes from our relationship with Jesus. First and most important, we are beloved and cherished children of God. Our sexuality is a minor facet of that identity as God's child, not the most important thing about us!

- **It's not our job to judge those outside the church.** Today's teenagers are taught to love and accept everyone—just as they should be! But a disequilibrium sets in when they try to decipher how they're supposed to act toward their gay friends. You can set them free from this by helping them embrace what Billy Graham famously said: "It is the Holy Spirit's job to convict, God's job to judge, and my job to love." And the apostle Paul tells us in 1 Corinthians 5:12 that we are not to judge those outside the church. This is a relief! Our primary job as followers of Jesus is to show love, acceptance, and support to those outside the church, no matter what.

- **The meaning of life is not found in romantic relationships.** What's the "happy message" of every romantic comedy ever made? Well, you'll encounter some wacky bumps in the road, but eventually you'll find your soulmate and (therefore) find the happiness you deserve. This is not the happy message (also called the "good news") that Jesus proclaimed. The good news we discover in the Bible is that God has redeemed his people through the life, death, and resurrection of Jesus Christ. When we surrender our lives to him, he invites us into a new life with him in his kingdom. The line between the "rom-com gospel" and the actual gospel can be fuzzy. That is, we unwittingly communicate that what matters *most* in life is to find your soulmate—and, yes, if you follow Jesus, you'll go to heaven when you die. God does call many into marriage, but *even in marriage* the purpose of our lives is to serve Jesus and others.

- **Jesus calls all of us to sacrifice in our sexuality.** The Bible envisions only two options for human sexual righteousness: a lifelong monogamous relationship between a man and a women, or celibacy. None of our sexual attractions are unblemished by the Fall. We're all tempted sexually, and we're all called to say no to actions that are outside God's boundaries out of reverence for him. A married man or woman vows to say no to sex with any but their spouse, just as a single Christian (whether gay or straight) is called to say no to acting on sexual temptation.

  While celibacy is, in some ways, more difficult than marriage, it's not impossible. Countless Christians for thousands of years have lived rich, fruitful, celibate lives. Pastor Ed Shaw, gay and celibate, argues in his book *Same-Sex Attraction and the Church: The Surprising Plausibility of the Celibate Life* that our culture's belief that satisfaction in life is rooted in a romantic relationship, whether gay or straight, is a lie. In general, churches are much better at supporting healthy marriages than they are at supporting healthy celibacy. The truth is, within a loving community of Jesus-followers, single people of all kinds can find full, meaningful lives as they pursue God's kingdom.

MINISTERING TO A GAY TEENAGER

When a student confides to you that he or she is gay, it's well worth your time to read *Ministering to Gay Teenagers* by Shawn Harrison or *Understanding Sexual Identity* by Mark Yarhouse. The topic is too important to address with inadequate preparation. These resources will certainly equip you. The crucial points include:

1. **Make sure gay teenagers know that Jesus cares for them, and so do you.** Students may wrongly assume there's something unredeemable about their desires or that you will reject them once they share this with you. Go out of your way to communicate that your support is unconditional.

2. **Give them time and space to work through this.** Because this issue is so complex and nuanced, these teenagers will need time to process it all. Give them the space to work through it, trusting in the Holy Spirit's direction. As Greg Coles, a celibate, gay Christian, writes in his memoir, "You can't just tell us what to believe and expect us to believe it. That's not how belief works." Give breathing room, not pressure.

3. **Confidentiality is key.** You'll want to keep your supervisor in the loop, but this is their story to tell their parents in their own time and in their own way. You'll likely cause an irreparable break in trust if they find out you told their parents without their knowledge.

Conversations about same-sex attraction are an important opportunity to talk about the Gospel. The only way a biblical understanding of sexuality will make sense to teenagers is if they understand the worth of Jesus and the goodness of God. Take them to passages like Mark 14, where the woman "wastes" the perfume on Jesus. It's not a waste at all, because Jesus is worth everything. Or Matthew 1, where Jesus compares the kingdom of God to the treasure in the field and the precious pearl. Remind them that *Jesus* is the treasure! When you find him, you find the most valuable thing in the universe.

4. Gender Identity—How do we talk with kids about gender-identity issues? We start with God's profound love for our created bodies. We are not disembodied spirits, and that's on purpose. The Bible says that God is spirit but he has deliberately chosen to give his children bodies. That means our bodies are important to Jesus; with them, we honor his will and express our love for him. God loves bodies so much that he chose to come to us in incarnate form—Jesus is a flesh-and-blood Messiah. It's important to remember that our spirits and bodies were created together: "You made all the delicate, inner parts of my body and knit me together in my mother's womb" (Psalm 139:13). God has given each of us a body tied to a specific gender because that body best serves the person he created us to be.

The important thing we need to tell our young people is that we believe God chose each of our genders for us and that our path to blessing will always lie in living into the choices he has made for us. Of course, this is another example of how our culture's understanding of gender identity contrasts so profoundly from the Bible's view that the context of God's goodness is essential. God wants the very best for his people; he wants us to thrive, and our path to thriving is found inside the gender he has selected for each of us. Again, two very helpful resources are *Understanding Gender Dysphoria* by Mark Yarhouse and *Love Thy Body* by Nancy Pearcey.

If you have students who are wrestling with their gender identity, here are some helpful guidelines:

1. **Emphasize that Jesus cares about them and you're committed to helping them wrestle with this issue.** There's nothing sinful about feeling uncomfortable with your gender. Most of us at some point feel like we don't really fit our culture's stereotype of the perfect man or perfect woman. It's helpful to emphasize that Jesus' teaching was never intended for perfect people. It's also important that they know they are fundamentally welcome in your group.

2. **Listen deeply, and be careful about your assumptions.** Some teenagers who are wrestling with gender identity struggle with negative feelings about their bodies—they don't think they fit the cultural stereotype for beauty. Others have recognized that their personality has characteristics that reflect the opposite gender more than their own. Still others are contemplating their gender identity in the wake of some kind of abuse. The goal is to understand specifically *why* teenagers are uncomfortable with their gender.

3. **There's a lot more flexibility in God's idea of "male" and "female" than we think.** Some males are sensitive and nurturing and uncomfortable with sports and other "boy things." Some females love sports and would've been called "tomboys" in the past. It's okay to be a man who has feminine traits and vice versa. Our culture's version of the ideal man and woman don't match God's ideals. It's fine to have some opposite-gender traits and live into those traits fully, as the gender we were born with.

4. **The Bible doesn't target transgenderism specifically.** We know that God has chosen to create us with bodies and that he has chosen to make us male or female, and it's the application of this principle that most helps us understand God's approach to transgenderism. The closest direct reference to gender identity is in Deuteronomy 22:5: "A woman must not put on men's clothing, and a man must not wear women's clothing." The verse speaks to the issue of women trying to appear as men and men trying to appear as women. But this reference is not the best way to help a young person understand biblical truth around gender identity. The body God has given each of us is no accident.

Conclusion

One of the exciting things about serving teenagers in ministry is that they're always asking questions. And one of the challenging things about serving teenagers in ministry is that they expect us to answer those questions. This chapter is a conversation-starter—a way of pointing you in the right direction so you can do your own research, talk to your ministry leaders, and figure out how to handle these issues in your context. And in case we haven't made this clear, small-group leaders aren't required to know the right answer to every question. It's always okay to answer a hard question with "I don't know, but I will find out and get back to you."

CHAPTER CODA

This Coda is Syler's "Beach Analogy" about how far is too far in sex and dating...

Imagine that I announce to my four small children that I want them to get their bathing suits on because we're going to the beach. I lather on the sunscreen, we gather up the sand toys, and we load up the minivan and head on our way. When we get to the beach, my children head straight for the water, but I stop them.

"Whoa, whoa, whoa!" I cry. "Who said anything about going in the water? I said we were going to the beach, but I never said we were going swimming!"

As you might imagine, my kids are not happy. The oldest pouts and says, "Dad, this is so stupid. Why did you do this to us? It's so hot...I want to swim!"

The next one begins to weep softly. "It's okay, Daddy. We don't have to swim," she says between sniffles. Such a sweet girl, but still, she's not happy.

The next one folds his arms in a determined pout pose. "Hmph! No! I want the water!!!"

My youngest then throws herself completely on her back and begins to scream and kick—it's a full-on tantrum. "Wat-uh! Wat-uh!!!!!"

Others look over at us, so I start to feel embarrassed. So I reason with myself, "I mean, we've gone to the trouble to come all the way down here, and the kids will be so happy if they get to swim. What will be the harm?"

So I turn to them and say, "Okay, kids...you can go in the water!" Cheers erupt. They wipe the tears off their faces and give me hugs. They begin to chant, "Daddy is the best! Daddy is the best!" They hold hands as they rush into the water.

And a giant sea monster comes out of the water and eats them all. The end.

What's the moral of the story?

If you've established a sexual boundary (nothing more than kissing, for example) and you think you can then go right up to the edge of that boundary without going past it, good luck with that. Don't get in the car and drive down to the beach and play on the edge of the water, because you *will* get in. That is, don't go down to the basement for a late-night make-out session and assume you will *only* make out. Come up with a better plan!

How to Answer Big Questions About God

(by Syler and Steven)

Teenagers have lots of hard questions, but most of them settle under a handful of broad themes. It's good to focus on those question-themes here. We're not delivering in-depth answers; we'll give you just enough to get you through a two-minute response. When these questions come up, it likely means that your teenagers are ready for more "meat." So invite them into a deeper exploration of the Bible's truths, either inside or outside your small group.

Here's our list of the top "big questions about God" we've heard from teenagers over the years, along with our approach to answering them.

1. How do we know God exists?

This is, of course, a fundamental question. We typically approach questions like this in one of two ways.

The first approach is to start with Jesus. Jesus believed in God. He claimed that he was God. Can we believe that? Did Jesus even really exist? This is not a debate among historians; they all believe he did exist. Jesus was a real person who lived 2,000 years ago in the land of Israel. So if he's real, can we believe what he said? If Jesus claimed to be God (John 8:56-58 and Mark 14:61-62, for example), it means he wasn't just a wise, excellent teacher. He was either a crazy person, incredibly deceptive, or actually who he said he was—God himself in human form. And if he was God himself, then yes, God exists.

Jesus did three things that confirm what he said was trustworthy: 1) He fulfilled dozens of prophecies in the Old Testament that predicted where he would live, how he would die, and even who he'd be related to. 2) He performed miracles and offered them as proof that he was trustworthy. 3) He rose from the dead. If Jesus himself is trustworthy, and the things he said are reliable, and he said there was a God, then we can believe it.

The second approach is to start with the "Big Bang." Many teenagers believe in the Big Bang theory commonly accepted in scientific circles: Before the universe that we know was formed, there was nothing. The matter in that *nothing* exploded and created planets and galaxies that formed and reformed into bigger ones. All that *nothing* finally evolved into the pinnacle of all existence, which we call the internet. ☺ How could all that just happen? Where did it all come from if it wasn't first created? Earth *works*. We need oxygen to breathe, and we emit carbon dioxide. Lucky for us, all the plants in the world take in that CO_2 and... what are the odds? They emit oxygen! Trees grow leaves that give us shade in the summer. Then the winter comes and the leaves fall, so we have something to do in October when we're bored—rake leaves. It actually takes more faith to believe that all this happened by accident than it does to believe in a God who created it.

2. Can we trust the Bible, and where did it come from?

Kids rightly want to know if the Bible they're reading is trustworthy. They see contrary views about this on the internet and in popular books and movies (remember *The Da Vinci Code*?). It's helpful, then, to know where it came from. Here are three helpful points:

- **The 27 books of the New Testament were prayerfully chosen by early church leaders.** Their process worked like this: There were lots of independent letters and accounts of Jesus' life floating around, from Paul's letters to the four Gospels we have today, plus other books like the Gospel of Thomas. The challenge was to figure out which of these books were completely reliable. A church in the first few centuries would've had handwritten copies of the books they considered divinely inspired, and each church compared their books with the books of other churches around them until a consensus developed about which of the books were *completely* inspired by God. Those are the 27 we have today.

- **The New Testament books we have today accurately represent what the original authors wrote.** Since that process all happened centuries ago, some people wonder if what we have today is still an accurate representation of all the original stories and letters, since it has been translated and rewritten multiple times. It turns out that there's a whole science that deals with ancient manuscripts, and the Bible is considered an ancient manuscript, as is Homer's *Iliad*. The scholars who study these manuscripts agree that the Bible we have today is substantially the same as what was written 2,000 years ago. This whole question was greatly helped in the 1940s when a shepherd in the Middle East stumbled on a cave containing copies of the books of the Old Testament that were probably put there about A.D. 70. The copies in the cave were virtually identical to the modern versions.

- **The history found in the New Testament squares with what historians and archaeologists agree is true.** To figure out if an ancient manuscript agrees with what we know of history, scientists compare the Bible to the writings of ancient historians and the findings of recent archaeological studies. The writings of famous historians like Flavius Josephus generally agree with what we find in the Bible, and the list of archaeological finds that agree with the Bible is pretty astonishing, including information about social customs, records of rulers mentioned in the Bible, and inscriptions that verify the existence of people mentioned in the Bible. What this means is that we can be confident that the Bible we read today is trustworthy, reliable, and historically accurate.

3. How do we know that our "religion" is the right one?

In our age of pluralism, it is the height of arrogance to assume that one religion is the "right" one and that others are missing the boat. The most popular viewpoint is that all religions basically teach the same thing. We're all just taking different roads up the same mountain. When we get to the top, we'll realize that we were all taking our own paths but we have ultimately arrived at the same destination.

The problem with this viewpoint is that it isn't intellectually accurate. While most religions do have some overlap in their beliefs, they do not all teach the same thing. Christianity says there is one God revealed in three persons. Hinduism holds to a belief in thousands of gods. Those both can't be true.

The reality is that there is only one religion that makes the radical claims of Christianity—namely, that God revealed himself in human form *uniquely*, in the person of Jesus Christ. Not only did Jesus claim to be God, but he proved it by performing miracles, fulfilling prophecies made in the Old Testament, and ultimately rising from the dead.

The point of the miracles is to provide supernatural evidence that Jesus is who he says he is. In John 14:11, Jesus says, "Just believe that I am in the Father and the Father is in me. Or at least believe because of the work you have seen me do." Paul claims as much when he says that when he came to the Corinthians, he "relied only on the power of the Holy Spirit...so [they] would trust not in human wisdom but in the power of God" (1 Corinthians 2:4-5). The Bible gives us example after example of miracles that validate Jesus' claims, culminating with his resurrection. But if kids are still skeptical, point them to miracles that happen today. With a quick search of the internet, you'll find examples of modern-day miracles. If you've never experienced one yourself, search for "Duane Miller Voice Miracle."

Think about it this way. If you're seriously injured and looking for a hospital, and a bunch of different people are telling you how to get there, it can be overwhelming and confusing. But if an ambulance arrives *from* the hospital and the driver says "Get in," you can trust it. Jesus is the rescuer that came from the hospital to save us. We can trust him.

4. If God is good, why is there pain and suffering?

This is a question that requires a much longer answer, but here are four points to spotlight:

- **The Bible is full of examples of godly people who suffer.** Starting with Adam and Eve (who experience one of their sons killing another) and continuing throughout the entire Old and New Testaments, suffering is present everywhere, ending only in John's vision of the new kingdom. When we suffer, we're only experiencing what people throughout the Bible (and human history) have lived through.

- **Suffering reminds us that Jesus, not us, is the center of the universe.** Many of us think that we're supposed to be immune from suffering. This is not the case everywhere in the world. In non-Western cultures in particular, people generally understand that life is full of joy *and* suffering and we should expect both. Life is hard, but God is good. But *we* figure that if God is good, then my life better be epic-awesome! Aren't we *owed* health and wealth and ease? But, in fact, Jesus doesn't promise us all that entitlement. Suffering reminds us that God's purposes are greater than ours.

As C.S. Lewis once said, "God whispers to us in our pleasures...but shouts in our pains. It is his megaphone to rouse a deaf world."

Peter tells us that the one who suffers in his body is done with sin (1 Peter 4:1). That is, when we suffer, the things that matter the most are the things we begin to care about. Everything is put into proper perspective. Suffering gets our attention in a way that nothing else does. It's a kind of portal to draw us closer to Jesus. When we see suffering as an obstacle to the pain-free life we think we're owed, we're revealing that God is not at the center of our universe.

- **Suffering allows us to be the hands and feet of Jesus to those who suffer.** Organizations such as International Justice Mission, Compassion, and World Vision have shown us what can happen when Christians follow Jesus' heart and come alongside those who are forgotten and marginalized. When we turn our attention away from ourselves and onto those considered the "least of these" (Matthew 25), we find Jesus.

- **Suffering points us to heaven.** We intellectually understand that heaven is our home, but not many of us live like it. In 2 Corinthians 4, Paul describes how our "present troubles are small and won't last very long. Yet they produce for us a glory that vastly outweighs them and will last forever!" But in the midst of our suffering, the pain sure doesn't feel small or momentary. But our sufferings do point us to that glorious time when all things will be made right. Joni Eareckson Tada was paralyzed in a diving accident and spent the ensuing 50 years in a wheelchair. She said this: "The dark despair of total and permanent paralysis that followed [my accident] wasn't much fun, but it sure made heaven come alive." Those who suffer understand more than anyone the hope of the life to come in God's kingdom (1 Corinthians 2:9).

5. How could a good God send someone (especially someone who has never heard of Jesus) to hell?

The topic of hell is incredibly challenging and confusing, but Jesus actually talked about it frequently. The hard part for our students is understanding how a loving, affectionate God who has sacrificed so much to invite us back into relationship could ever condemn someone to an eternity of torture. Add to that the question about people who've never had a chance to hear about Jesus, and it sounds even more unfair. Here are three important ideas, rooted in Scripture, to communicate on this topic when your teenagers ask:

- **It's God's desire that everyone would choose him.** In 2 Peter 3:9, the apostle reaffirms Jesus' desire for all people to put their faith in him. We start with an understanding that God takes no delight in the death of wicked people (Ezekiel 33). He wants each person to make decisions that will lead to life.

- **Jesus gives us the freedom to reject him.** As people with the ability to make our own choices, it is up to us to either choose or reject Jesus' offer of forgiveness. And here's where the question of those who've never heard comes into play. Romans 1 says that God's invisible qualities can clearly be seen so people have no excuse. In other words, God has made his existence known everywhere, through all of creation.

  C.S. Lewis' view on this is helpful. In *The Problem of Pain*, he imagines hell as a place where God has allowed people to exist without forcing his way into their lives. So hell collects selfish people together, apart from God's presence or influence, and the way they treat each other turns it into torture. He says the lock on the door of hell is on the inside, not the outside. Elsewhere Lewis says, "There are only two kinds of people in the end: those who say to God, 'Thy will be done,' and those to whom God says, in the end,

'Thy will be done.' All that are in Hell, choose it. Without that self-choice there could be no Hell. No soul that seriously and constantly desires joy will ever miss it. Those who seek find. [To] those who knock it is opened." The doctrine of hell is, in fact, rooted in the mercy of God and his desire to give us the freedom to choose him or reject him.

- **It's none of your business who goes to hell.** Don't get worked up by speculative worries about who might or might not be saved. Those of us who are in Christ have the assurance that we will be with him forever. So we live for heaven while doing all we can to point others that way. Psalm 98:9 is illuminating: "He will judge the world with justice and the nations with fairness." All God's judgments will be done with righteousness and fairness. Jesus loves even those who've never heard of him, and he is the inventor of the concept of justice. We don't need to wonder or worry if he will be fair; that's who he is.

6. Is abortion wrong?

Abortion is a difficult issue and a lightning rod for strong opinions. This is one of those questions where pastoral concerns need to come before theological concerns. The first thing to determine is why the question is being asked. Has the teenager had an abortion, or does she know someone who's about to? If the answer is yes, then we first listen and ask questions.

When it's time to talk about the theology, here are the essential points:

- **God values human life that is developing in the womb** (Exodus 21:22-25).

- **God is, in fact, the one who forms human life inside the mother** (Psalm 139:13-16).

- **God knows us and has plans for us even before he forms us in the womb** (Jeremiah 1:5).

A teenager's view about abortion is related to his or her views about sex. One who chooses to obey God's design for sex as only between a husband and wife won't have to face this issue (except in the very rare case of rape). The next step involves how to live out this belief: with love and compassion for those who may disagree with us. The best response we can encourage in our kids is to work toward a lifestyle of valuing life in every context we find it—the unborn, yes, but also people with intellectual disabilities, the poor, the elderly, and others who society pushes to the margins. We need a robust theology of caring for life in every facet.

Conclusion

It's important when discussing these questions that we actually show our teenagers where in the Bible to find the relevant verses. Our only trustworthy source for the answers we've given here is the Bible, and excellent small-group leaders take every opportunity to direct their kids to the Bible and to the Jesus of the Bible.

CHAPTER CODA

This is a true story about Syler and his son Foster, when Foster was about 3 years old...

I was in my office at the end of a Sunday morning, and I was about to take Foster home when he looked at me and said, "Dad, when are you gonna take God out of the box?"

"Hold on. What did you say to me, bud?"

"When are you gonna take God out of the box?"

I stopped and stared at him. What was going on? Was God speaking to me through my 3-year-old son? Had I been putting God in a box? Was I limiting God's power, unwilling to allow him to fully unleash his work in my life and ministry?

With desperation in my eyes, ready to fall on my knees and repent of my lack of faith, I asked him, "What do you mean, bud?"

He then pointed to the Jesus Action Figure that a student had recently given me, which was prominently displayed on my bookshelf. He had learned in the children's ministry that Jesus was God, and he obviously knew what Jesus looked like (beard, long hair, robe), and he wanted to play with the Jesus that was still in its box.

I was relieved but also a little sad that God wasn't speaking to me supernaturally. My son just wanted to play with a toy.

Still...don't put God (or Jesus) in a box. And let your kids play with your toys. My son is still bitter about that one.

How to Maintain Healthy Boundaries

(by Syler)

A good friend of mine worked at a church in the Pacific Northwest where they hired a youth ministry intern (I'll call him Brad) from a local seminary. Brad had a heart for students on the fringe and began spending time with a teenager from a broken home who was using drugs. They began a friendship, and Brad decided he would do *anything* to help this young man quit his drug use and find salvation in Jesus. One night, the teenager told Brad, "I'll stop using drugs if you smoke pot with me." Incredibly, Brad was so focused on helping this kid that he agreed to do it. The student then blackmailed Brad into getting a hotel room for him and his friends so they could get drunk. Eventually, Brad confessed everything to his church leaders. The teenager accused him of molestation. He ended up spending a year in jail.

Unfortunately, when we ignore healthy boundaries in our relationships with teenagers, our best intentions can take a nasty turn.

Close relationships are the goal of good youth ministry, and that means inappropriate relationships are one of our greatest occupational hazards. When we move beyond polite youth ministry, walls fall down and the line between leader and friend can get blurry. Platonic feelings can morph into romantic feelings. Romantic feelings carry shame with them, and suddenly a thriving ministry can descend into a real mess.

Here are 10 things to consider:

1. Be accountable. One of the most important relationships we can have in youth ministry is an accountability partner—ideally, someone who's involved in our ministry and knows how we interact with our students. Someone who can ask hard questions and challenge us. We need to be comfortable sharing potentially embarrassing things with this person. In Proverbs 27:17, Solomon says, "As iron sharpens iron, so a friend sharpens a friend." We must be iron for each other. Choose someone who will actually hold you to your commitments and won't be afraid to call you out when necessary.

2. Let Jesus, not ministry, meet your needs. Two questions to continually ask ourselves in our interactions with teenagers are "Where am I getting my 'needs' met?" and "Am I ministering out of a place of wholeness in Jesus, or am I turning to these students to make me feel good about myself?"

In general, volunteer leaders should spend the bulk of their time and interaction with kids of the same gender. In some settings, this is impractical. In all situations, we must be sure we're reaching out to kids in an emotionally healthy way. A youth leader friend told me about a time he was involved in a ministry that required him to be in communication with a group of high school girls. Even though his relationship with these teenagers was healthy, he was on a business trip when he realized that his first impulse at the end of a busy day was to check in with those girls, not his wife. Without realizing it, he'd fallen into an emotionally needy relationship with these teenagers. Be aware that when you are tired or upset, the temptation to "extract life" from your kids will be stronger.

3. Discern the line between leader and friend. As a small-group leader, you absolutely want to be a friend to your kids; you want them to trust you, and you want to trust them. But you're much more than just their friend. Brad forgot this line, and he paid the price. It's tricky, but it's essential that you assume the role of leader, not a peer or friend.

4. **Be aware of the Messiah Complex.** Brad had a "Messiah Complex." He thought he could be a teenager's Savior, the "chosen one" who had the power to turn this student into a disciple. It's easy to fall into this trap because we all want to reach kids with Jesus' radical love. I've read plenty of powerful stories about youth workers who went to extreme measures to be there for kids in difficult situations. Passion for our mission can make it very easy to lose our perspective. There's a fine line between showing someone radical love in a healthy way and losing track of appropriate boundaries in a relationship. We must be able to say, "I'm sorry, I care about you, but no, I'm not going to do that."

Kids who have difficult home lives are more challenging. It's tempting to jump in and fix their problems, and they often don't have good boundaries modeled for them at home. Understand that you can only do what you can do. Once, when I was in high school, I was at my pastor's house when he was finishing up a phone call with a parishioner. I didn't know what was going on, but I remember he said this: "Well, here's the deal, I actually *can't* help you, but I can point you to a Savior who can." Bottom line: Jesus is the Messiah; we aren't.

5. **Be vigilant on social media and in digital interactions with teenagers.** Every volunteer leader must be aware of his or her social media presence. Assume that both teenagers and their parents will be reading everything you post. Social media can be a great way to interact with kids, as long as everything is aboveboard and appropriate. When you become a small-group leader, your social media accounts fold into your ministry. Ask yourself, "Would I want my teenagers or their parents to view what I'm posting?"

6. **Beware of inappropriate attachments.** Another friend was ministering to a young woman in a tough home situation. At some point, he began to develop an emotional attachment to her, and he didn't know what to do about it. Thankfully, this story didn't end badly. My friend told his supervisor about his feelings and stopped spending time with her.

But he said his feelings really came out of nowhere—he was ambushed by them. He felt like he was a terrible person and wondered how he could possibly be qualified for ministry in light of his feelings. The reality is that it *does* happen, and it doesn't mean you're a creep or a weirdo. Simply make sure you drag your feelings into the light before they turn into actions. The destructive power of these relationships is fueled by shame: "What would people think if they heard I had a crush on a high school girl? I'd better not tell anyone."

When we listen to the shame of accusation (shame is never from Jesus, by the way), it pushes our feelings deeper into the darkness, where they grow in strength. Freedom comes when we bring the relationship into the light. The best way to diminish the power of any inappropriate feelings you have is to share them with a trusted friend or ministry leader—someone who can keep you accountable. It's certainly not healthy to have a crush on a teenager, but it could happen.

Sometimes it's easier for others to recognize these crushes. I may think, "Oh there's nothing going on here. Jesus is just moving through me to impact his or her life." If we can accept these warnings from others nondefensively, we can save ourselves before anything begins.

I learned a lot from Steven early on when he'd talk about "little crushes." He never joked about it; it was clear that "crushes" were dangerous. But he also didn't brand these feelings as the "unforgivable sin." If there's a culture of openness among your leaders, you can help each other.

It reminds me of a famous passage from C.S. Lewis' *The Great Divorce* (one of my favorite passages in all of literature). A ghost-man is visiting heaven. He has a little red lizard sitting on his shoulder, which is obviously keeping him from entering into glory. An angel offers to kill the lizard, and the lizard frantically reminds the man of why this would be a bad idea. Finally, the man relents and allows the lizard to be killed. He is suddenly free of his shame. The lizard then turns into a beautiful stallion, and the ghost turns into a real man and rides the stallion into heaven.

The lizard of shame will plead for its life and beg us not to kill it. But it must be killed. And when it dies, it morphs into the freedom we need.

7. Be careful on youth trips. Leaders naturally spend more time with teenagers of the opposite sex during camps and mission trips. I heard a story about a leader who had an affair with another leader on a mission trip. It was told with utter incredulity: "On a mission trip...can you believe that?!" Actually, that makes perfect sense. When you share an intense, physically demanding experience like a mission trip, camp, or retreat, your walls come down. When your guard is relaxed, it's easy to allow temptation to find a foothold.

8. Understand that kids can crush on you. Students have crushes on older people all the time. It happens with teachers, and it happens with ministry leaders as well. Be aware of this dynamic, and help guard *students'* hearts by not acting in a flirtatious way. You don't want to cause any confusion. Some people are naturally bubbly and friendly, but their demeanor can be perceived as flirty by others. This is when we need others around us to let us know when our "friendly" is crossing the line into "flirty." Because we're focused on the ministry "fruit" in the relationship, it's easy to miss this dynamic; we assume the teenager is simply responding to our guidance and teaching.

9. Make sure kids know you'll say no. We want to communicate that we're available to our teenagers, but it's important for them to experience our boundaries. My wife and I always want the teenagers in our group to feel like they can stop by our house any time, but there are times we need to *not* be available. So if our exterior light is on, kids know we are "open for business." If the light is off, we're "closed." If there's an emergency, by all means call me. But short of that, my family's health requires off-duty times.

10. Advocate for background checks and sexual-abuse prevention training. As a volunteer, you have no control over this, but if no one has done a background check on you, you need to ask why not. Shepherdswatch.com is a good place to start. This is just too important to be overlooked.

CHAPTER CODA

Nothing fancy this time. Just a little biblical wisdom... Proverbs 7 is a warning against marital unfaithfulness. We can adapt this warning to our behavior in youth ministry. I've paraphrased the final four verses for that purpose:

Proverbs 7:24-27 (ESV—Edited Syler Version)

Now then, my youth leaders, let me tell you something. No, seriously, like I need EYEBALLS here. Thanks. Don't let your heart be drawn away from your commitment, and don't walk down the wrong path. Unfortunately, there's a pile of bodies you'll be walking over; I mean, it's really depressing how many. Straying from righteousness in this way basically means your life is over; you're as good as dead.

There's no reason youth ministry should land anyone in jail. Be wise! You can do this.

How to Understand Adolescence, and Why It Matters

(by Steven)

I have a vivid memory from my first youth group that involves Syler. We were on a 24-hour bus ride from Texas to Colorado for a ski trip. We had a bus-full of teenagers, and we were all tired and grumpy—*so* ready for that ride to be over. I could not keep middle school Syler from jumping into the aisle of the bus to coax the whole bus into singing show tunes. For the adults it was irritating (except for my future wife, who loved show tunes and thought Syler was hilarious). For the high schoolers it was almost intolerable. He came within seconds of tragically ending his brilliant youth ministry career before it ever started.

On that bus trip, we could see glimmers of the intelligent, entertaining adult Syler would become. He'd figured out that he had a gift for making people laugh. He knew he could perform and people would pay attention. Unfortunately, he hadn't yet developed an adult's ability to read the mood of the people around him and, therefore, was utterly oblivious to those on the bus who (with that one exception) wanted to kill him.

Syler was going through early adolescence—that period of transition between childhood and adulthood when young people are changing faster physically, mentally, and socially than at any time of life since their infancy. In some ways, he could already function as the adult he would become; in other ways, he was still a child. The dissonance was jarring.

It's almost impossible for us to refrain from evaluating our teenagers the same way we evaluate the adults around us. But these kids aren't adults. Understanding their developmental journey can help us understand why they do the things they do and how to respond to them in a way that makes them feel more loved and valued.

1. Teenagers are in transition.

Adolescents aren't children anymore, but they're also not yet adults. They stopped being children when puberty started (usually around 10 or 11) and won't generally be considered adults until they have jobs, have spouses, and have moved out of their parents' houses.

This season of life is notoriously difficult for most people. I remember the years of middle school and high school as some of the most confusing, stressful years of my life. That's probably true for you, and it's helpful to realize that it's probably true for your teenagers. Sometimes they act like adults—they can be gracious, considerate, insightful, and thoughtful. And then in the next second...

2. Teenagers sometimes act like children.

...They can be selfish, impulsive, whiny, and undependable. But they *hate* it when you treat them like children. At the same time, if you treat them like adults, they'll frequently let you down. Once, I tried to go to lunch with one of my students. We set up the date. I put it on my calendar. I showed up...and he didn't. Completely forgot. If an adult did that to me without a good excuse, I would assume they weren't interested in spending time with me. That's not what it means when my teenagers forget something important. Their brains aren't fully developed, and they have lots of chaos flying around in there. I've learned that even when they desperately want to meet with me, I must take responsibility for making sure they don't forget. That's because I'm the adult, and they're not yet. So I set the meeting, I remind them the week before, and I remind them the night before.

3. Teenagers are stuck "in between" for a long time.

I'm sure you've seen a movie or read a book that explores the "coming of age" theme. In its primitive form, the elders of the village recognize that childhood is ending, so the child leaves the protection of the village to undergo a "transition" ordeal—a night spent alone or a quest to kill and eat an adult bear. When the young person returns, he or she is recognized as an adult. This is called a rite of passage, marking the movement from one period of life to another. In some early societies, the transition was brief. One day you were a child, and the next night or week you're recognized as a (bear-stuffed) adult.

In contemporary Western culture, we don't have a single rite of passage marking the transition from childhood to adulthood. Instead, we have about 20 that are stretched out over a 15-year period. Here are just a few:

- Confirmation at 13
- Driver's license at 16
- High school graduation at 18
- Legally allowed to drink at 21
- College graduation at 22
- Marriage at 28 or 29

In our society, people stop being children between 10 and 13 years old but then don't really become adults for about 15 years. No wonder it's such a confusing time!

4. Teenagers are changing fast.

This is a time of radical change. Kids' bodies are growing rapidly. They're getting bigger and stronger even as their brains develop the ability to think and explore in completely new (adult) ways. These changes, in turn, lead to whole new ways of relating to the people around them.

5. Teenagers have bodies that confuse them.

Middle school kicks off an intense season of physical growth, the fastest since infancy. During puberty alone, guys will grow about 8 inches in height and gain 15 pounds. Girls will grow 3 inches and gain almost 20 pounds! Guys go through a clumsy stage as they try to master their bigger bodies, right about the time they're suffering through the embarrassment of their voices changing. Girls witness their bodies packing on fat around their hips and breasts, just when they start to figure out that our society's idea of beauty is ultra-slim. This is the reason so many young women develop eating disorders around this time. And if all that isn't enough, a hurricane of hormones has brought on a sea-change of confusing new feelings and fascinations.

6. Teenagers have brains that are developing superpowers.

At the same time their bodies are growing, teenagers' brains are actually growing new hardware, giving them new capacity to think abstractly. Abstract thinking facilitates at least two important new abilities: They can discern what other people are thinking by imagining life from their perspective, and they can appreciate and understand metaphors.

Back to the story about Syler that opened this chapter. His inability to see himself from another's point of view was the reason he was almost thrown out of a moving bus. He could not imagine how the older students were perceiving him, so he had no idea that he was *really* bothering them.

The inability to understand metaphor can be just as limiting. For example, we led a lesson with our high schoolers in which we read through the story of Mary and Joseph around the manger. We assigned roles from the story, read through it a section at a time, and asked the teenagers to tell us what their characters were feeling and thinking at that point. It was powerful. New insights about the Scripture and God popped up in almost every answer. It was so great that my volunteer leaders wanted to do the same thing with our middle schoolers.

We set up everything the same way. Same story, same roles—we were even in the same room. We read the story the same way and asked the same questions. And we got...nothing. Blank stares. The middle schoolers seemed lost because they couldn't see life through the eyes of another person. This is one reason interactive and experiential learning is so crucial in youth ministry; it's a flexible way to engage teenagers across the developmental span. When you're pursuing questions and discovering truths in conversation with others, and when you're experiencing a truth, not just talking about it, the environment is "rich soil" for growth. Think about how we tend to over-explain aspects of our faith, in contrast with how often Jesus used experiences, conversation, story, and metaphor to teach truth.

7. Teenagers are experiencing upheaval in their social worlds.

At the same time that all these physical and mental changes are going on, teenagers' social worlds are changing radically. In childhood, Mom and Dad are the most influential people in their lives. Now all they seem to care about is their friends. Their entire world rises or falls based on their friend-group and who has said or done what to whom.

It's also at this point that most teenagers form close-knit constellations of friends that sociologists call "primary groups." Teenagers increasingly base their beliefs and their actions on the beliefs and actions of the others in their primary group. You can probably remember who your small group of best friends was during this period. Mine were Richard and John. We did everything together. Now, decades later, we still see each other once a year.

It's important to understand your kids' primary groups because youth ministry is really all about reaching primary groups. If one member of a primary group attends your group, the others may be close behind. Primary groups can morph into cliques, so it's helpful to have them on your radar.

8. Teenagers are trying to figure out who they are.

Developmental psychologists say that one of the most important things going on inside adolescents is the formation of an adult identity. Our kids are trying to figure out who and what they are. If you spend time around middle school and early high school students, you can see them trying on various identities to find something that fits. It can be very frustrating to see them acting completely different depending on what group of people they're with. It's through relationships that teenagers figure out who they are.

This is one of the reasons your small group is so valuable to them. If it's working well, they'll have a group of Christian friends with a caring adult who can help them understand who Jesus made them to be. You (as their caring adult mentor) and the other teenagers in your group are two of the critical Relational Pillars of Adolescent Faith that we spotlighted in the first chapter. These pillars become more and more important the older they get. And that brings us to the final Important-Thing-to-Know-About-Teenagers point...

9. Teenagers are developing a faith that's no longer borrowed from their parents' faith.

Their faith is changing rapidly. In childhood, faith in Christ is mainly based on their parents' example and is limited by their inability to think about faith abstractly. In their teenage years they can think about things differently. They'll often start to question things about God they'd always taken for granted. Their parents' opinions are still important but are no longer the final word. If you're open to their questions, your small group can be a helpful, supportive place for them to form a healthy adolescent faith in Jesus.

10. Teenagers need "Three Relational Pillars" to continue maturing toward an adult faith.

This more personal adult faith that our adolescents are trying to grasp is built on three essential relationships that I call the Three Relational Pillars of adolescent faith.

- **The first, unsurprisingly, is their relationships with other Jesus-following peers.** For teenagers to have a faith that is healthy and growing, they need a set of friends they can share their faith with—peers they can struggle/pray/discuss/argue/share with as they discover the role faith will play as they grow into adulthood. This is why a small group plays such a crucial role in their maturing faith. It give kids access to close Christian peer relationships.

- **The next relational pillar is Christian mentors—older adults in church who spend time with them.** Sometimes this pillar includes coaches or older peers, but (surprisingly) it rarely includes parents. When we ask, "Overall, who in your life has had the biggest influence on your faith?" about half of Christians will say "my parents." But if you ask specifically, "Who in your life was the biggest influence on your faith during high school or college?" very few point to their parents. As one of my students said, "My parents were essential; they just weren't central." Teenagers desperately need mentors! As a small-group leader, you have a rare opportunity to make a lifelong difference in your teenagers' faith lives.

- **The third relational pillar is a relationship with Jesus himself.**
  When I say our students need a personal relationship with Jesus,
  I mean that they need some sort of direct encounter with God. As
  adults, we don't often talk about these encounters, but they are
  far more widespread than we believe and far more important to
  adolescent faith than we assume. For many, they mark a crucial
  turning point in their faith lives. You hear about these turning
  points frequently in teenagers' faith testimonies. Most include some
  version of "I went to church all my life, but I didn't really believe
  until I had an encounter with Jesus at this retreat I went on." That
  encounter might be described as "hearing God's voice" or "feeling
  his love for me" or "I just couldn't stop crying." It's a crucial turning
  point or two that involves a direct, memorable experience with
  God. This is why we so emphasize the importance of retreats,
  mission trips, and conferences. They're an on-ramp into these
  essential encounters with Jesus.

Conclusion

The more you know about the kids in your small group, the better you
can care for them. So remember, they are in an in-between time of life,
poised uncomfortably between childhood and adulthood, and they need
lots of patience. They're growing fast, with physical, mental, and social
changes all happening at the same time. And they're questioning their
faith in ways they never have before.

It's in your small group that they can start to live out close
relationships with Christian peers and benefit from your attention and
mentorship. It's in your small group that they can seek answers for
questions that have never occurred to them before. The reasons it's
difficult to be a teenager are also the reasons ministry to teenagers is so
important and so fruitful. Your small group can be literally life-changing.

CHAPTER CODA

Probably, all this talk about adolescence has made you hungry! As promised, then, here is Syler's world-famous pumpkin bread recipe, enjoyed by his family for generations (long before the Pumpkin Spice craze).

  2 c. whole wheat flour
  1½ c. white flour
  1½ t. salt
  2 t. baking soda
  1 t. nutmeg
  1 t. cinnamon
  3 c. sugar
  1 c. oil
  4 eggs
  ⅔ c. water
  1 can pumpkin

Mix dry ingredients together and set aside. Combine sugar and wet ingredients and mix well. Gradually add flour mixture and mix well. Makes two regular-size loafs or eight mini-loafs. Can be made into muffins as well. Bake at 350 degrees for 50 minutes. The very center of large loaf pans will be somewhat gooey, but don't overbake the edges.

Make pumpkin bread for your small group—teenagers eat everything.

How to Help Your Teenagers Take Important Next Steps

(by Syler)

My life changed forever during my senior year in high school. Up until then, I was a typical suburban teenager. I was a nice little honors student who loved going to youth group because that's where my friends were. At a Young Life-type summer camp, I invited Jesus into my heart, but I wouldn't say I had much of a relationship with him. Jesus was there just to help me reach my goals in life (namely, to become a successful actor) and to bail me out when I got in trouble. I was living life from a Syler-centric worldview. Why? Because I didn't actually believe that Jesus wanted more from me. I was Exhibit A for the term that Christian Smith and Melinda Lundquist Denton famously coined years later: a Moralistic Therapeutic Deist. My relationship with Jesus was polite and distant. I was not, in fact, a disciple.

So what changed? First, *my experience with Jesus* changed. Music was a big deal in our youth group, and I was part of "the band"—a row of acoustic guitar players sitting on a bench. This was a crucial opportunity for my friends and me to participate, not just spectate. But the music itself was not what I would call "worship"; we were singing songs *about* Jesus but not *to* Jesus.

My senior year, I quit doing theater at school because (surprise, surprise) the drama department at my high school had a little too much drama. So I accepted an invitation to be a leader for the middle school youth group, led by a volunteer leader named Steven Tighe. In our leader meetings, we sang new songs that had a much different feel to them, songs sung *to* God: "Good to Me" and "Oh How I Need You, Lord." These songs invited us in to powerful, intimate moments with a living God. And as we drew near to him in worship, we could tell he was drawing near to us.

That was Step One in my path toward discipleship. Step Two was understanding that *the miracles we read about in the Bible still happen*. In John 14:12, Jesus promised his disciples that they'd do the same (and greater) things than he was doing. Around this time I went on my first international mission trip to Monterrey, Mexico, where we performed dramas and did door-to-door Bible distribution. On that trip my faith became an active thing for me, something that made sense only when it was lived out.

In the spring of my senior year, my Syler-centric view of faith finally shifted forever. One night at a retreat I was helping lead, it just kind of clicked. It hit me for the first time in my life that the point of life is not for Jesus to help me but for me to serve him and join him in his mission to "set captives free." The change in my life was immediate. I remember coming back from the retreat thinking, "I don't need to be famous anymore. Who needs fame from *people* when the Creator of the universe knows my name?" Someone could have taught me that lesson, sure, but only Jesus could've written it on my heart.

My growing faith thrived in college, where I began to see God move in powerful ways. I could sense his guiding hand in the decisions I was making. I was bold in letting others know that my faith in Jesus was the most important thing in my life. I did an evangelistic Bible study at my theater school and had all sorts of people come hang out in the courtyard to study the Bible, smoke cigarettes (them, not me), and ask questions about who Jesus was. From time to time, when we heard about someone who needed physical healing, we would pray for them. And sometimes they were healed. As college came to a close, my desire to be involved in theater waned and my desire to pursue ministry grew. Had I not had these encounters with God, my faith would've continued as an add-on to my Syler-centric life, and eventually it would've become a footnote.

Over the years, I've seen similar stories play out in my students' lives. Here are my four big takeaways:

1. Connect with your teenagers outside of small group.

The more time we spend with kids, the greater our influence will be. My life changed forever when I started hanging out more deliberately with Steven. Since we can only do so much during a small-group time, the easiest way to expand our influence is to grab a meal or coffee with them. This might feel awkward at first, but remember what's on the other side of awkward? Yeah, that's right. Awesome is waiting. What may mitigate some of that awkwardness is hanging out with more than one at a time. As you get to know them more, it will feel much more organic, and your time together will become more meaningful.

- **Go to their sports events and performances, ideally with other small-group members.** If it's a sports event, you don't have to stay for the whole thing—even 30 minutes makes a big impact. If you can make a connection with a parent who's there, that's even better. As a parent of teenagers, I can't tell you how significant it is to see my son's leader at a school event. I know they aren't *excited* about watching my kid swim the hundred-meter backstroke. That's boring even for me. But it communicates two things: They care about my son, and they are my allies.

- **Plan a group gathering—it's an important way for the group to bond.** Here's my advice: Talk to the three or four teenagers who are the most committed, ask them what they'd like to do, and then plan an event that works with their schedule. *Then* let the rest of the group know. If only those few show up, it will feel like the event was a win, regardless of who else comes.

- **Remember this imperative:** *Do for the one what you wish you could do for the group.* Years ago, I had a group of senior guys who were incredible. Each one was poised to be a sensational leader, and I knew if I could spend time with them outside of our small group, they could grow even more. But there were seven of them. I knew I didn't have time to intentionally mentor each one outside of our small-group time, so I didn't pursue any of them. That was a mistake. I should've done for even one of them what I wish I could've done for all of them. You know that cheesy starfish analogy? An old man sees a boy on a starfish-covered beach throwing them back in the ocean one at a time. The old man laughs at him and tells him it won't make any difference. The boy picks up one more, throws it in the ocean, and says, "Well, it made a difference to that one."

- **Make yourself available to every teenager in your group, but intentionally pour into one or two of them to help them grow to spiritual maturity**. How do you choose? That's an imperfect science. Maybe you see exceptional potential. Maybe one of them pursues you. Don't apologize for investing in one or two more deeply, but don't broadcast it either.

Jesus did this. He had 12 disciples (a pretty good size for a small group), but then he had the three he invested more of himself in (Peter, James, and John). Of those three, he told only Peter that he was building his church on him. We pour our lives into the one (or two or three, if we have capacity) and see what God does.

2. Find ways for your teenagers to lead.

When kids are older and one or two have demonstrated both the ability and the interest to handle more responsibility, invite them to help lead. For my second-semester senior groups in particular, I encourage our leader to give the reins to a different senior each week. It may be hard for us to watch as kids struggle to lead, but it'll be so good for them. First, they'll see how hard it is to be in your shoes. Second, it will force them to prepare like they've never done before. Third, it may cause their peers to respond differently than if you were leading. Keep in mind that you'll need to meet with student leaders briefly before your meeting to make sure they know what they're doing and what you expect.

As I mentioned, my own faith blossomed when I was a teenager leading a group of middle schoolers. When I was telling these kids that they should read their Bibles, it occurred to me that maybe *I* should read *my* Bible. And I did. When the bar was raised for me, I responded.

Regularly point out the strengths and gifts you see in your teenagers. Many will not see their leadership potential themselves. They need someone like you to point it out to them. Jon Ferguson calls this the "ICNU" concept—we describe to others what "I see in you..." Often we will see leadership skills in others before they see them in themselves. Call others into leadership, even before they feel "ready."

Matt Redman is a prolific worship leader whose pastor, Mike Pilavachi, tells a story about the first time Matt led worship. He ended a song by pumping his fist in the air and yelling "Yeah!" Mike said it was awful, but "Matt had to be a *bad* worship leader before he could be a *good* one." That will often be true for our kids as they learn to lead, and it's worth it! No one shows up perfectly formed.

I go through a five-step process with new leaders:

1. I do, you watch.

2. I do, you help.

3. You do, I help.

4. You do, I watch.

5. You do, someone else watches.

This process is hard to get perfect. Sometimes we're too controlling, and we leave the new leader stuck in step two. Other times we want to skip ahead to step four, and they aren't ready. A few years ago, we were trying to get a freshman (Joe) trained to play bass in the worship band. He had lots of raw talent but didn't always come prepared. Our leader tried to jump too quickly to step four without taking him through one, two, and three. That led to an unintentional Step 2.5—you think you're "doing," but what you're hearing is me "doing" in the storage closet behind the sound booth. That is to say, on the night Joe was set to play, he wasn't ready, but my leader felt bad telling him he wasn't good enough. So he asked one of our other musicians to sit in the storage closet and play the parts. Joe *thought* he was playing, and so did everyone else, but only three of us knew the truth. So don't be lazy and skip the steps!

My last bit of advice: When someone brings a new idea, focus on "wow-ing" their idea instead of "how-ing" it. Even if it's a crazy idea that has zero chance of working, our first response needs to be "Wow!" That communicates that we believe in them and encourages them to dream. If the idea is bad, the teenager will figure that out at some point on his or her own.

When you invite your kids to lead, their lives change.

3. Make it normal for your teenagers to seek God's movement in miraculous ways.

I saw a cartoon with a dad and his daughter in front of a roller coaster. The daughter is saying to her dad, "It's okay, Dad, we're not at church. You can raise your hands here." There was a time, especially when that cartoon was published, when there was a significant divide between hand-raisers and non-hand-raisers. If you went to a hand-raiser church, that also likely meant that you had identified yourself as a card-carrying "charismatic." And the non-hand-raisers had their own set of doctrines. What I observe today in young people is that they just want more of Jesus. They want his kingdom to come, and they care less about the categories.

When a friend of mine was in high school, a girl in his youth group was diagnosed with cancer. The church he went to didn't talk about praying for sick people, and unbeknownst to him, it was a controversial issue. But he had been reading his Bible and thought it was pretty obvious what needed to happen: They needed to do what Jesus would do, which is pray for the girl to be healed. So he organized a group of people to lay hands on her and asked God to heal her, just like he read about in the Gospels. And you know what? She was healed. He didn't overthink it. He didn't stop to ask himself what the theological implications were. He just responded in the way he thought Jesus would respond.

The issue of praying for healing is complicated, of course, because there are many times we pray for healing and it doesn't come. Jesus told us to pray for healing, but in this "already-but-not-yet" time we live in, not everyone will be healed. There's a day ahead when we'll see the kingdom fully revealed and everyone will be healed, but that time hasn't come yet. With that caveat, we can unleash our kids to follow Jesus in bold ways. And we need to model that in our actions, too.

If we believe that Jesus is still moving in power in our lives today, then don't overthink it. Just act, and invite your teenagers to do the same. Ask God to speak to you, and when you think he has, respond. Ask God to heal the sick, and even if they aren't healed, keep praying. Let your kids catch you believing in a God who is active and present in the lives of his children. When you model it, they'll respond. In fact, sometimes, they'll go way beyond your modeling.

That's exactly what happened once when I took my teenagers to a conference...

4. Use events such as mission trips, retreats, and conferences to push the envelope.

For Steven's Ph.D. research, he talked to young adults who grew up in the church and still had a strong faith. Almost every one of them listed a direct encounter with God as a very important component to their faith development. And in almost every story, those encounters took place at a camp, conference, retreat, or mission trip. When possible, find opportunities for extended times away with your kids.

Most years, I take our student ministry team to a missions conference near my hometown in Texas. I do it because I want to move my teenagers out of their comfort zone, to see how Jesus is moving in other places. To be honest, it can make me uncomfortable. That's why they call it a "comfort zone"–because of how comfy-cozy it is. But this experience challenges their status quo in a way nothing else does. Especially the one year when we signed up for a "Power Encounter" breakout session.

The speaker, a friend of mine, began telling stories about how he has been in everyday situations (a grocery store or a park, for instance) where the Spirit speaks to him with specific details about a stranger's life, and he feels the Spirit urging him to go ask that person about those details and offer to pray. Then he said, "And when we're done with this session, we're gonna send everyone out to do the same thing."

I was familiar with this kind of thing before but didn't know how my kids would react. I was readying myself with reasons we could sit this one out when a teenager turned to me and said, "Sy, do we need to listen to the rest of the message?" *I know, this makes me uncomfortable too,* I thought.

But before I could say, "Yeah, this is pretty weird; we can duck out early if you want to," she followed up by saying, "We want to get started praying for people. Can we go *now*?!"

What sort of awful youth pastor was I that I wanted to leave early so we could retreat back into our comfort zone? All my kids wanted was to leave early so they could go listen to God and pray for strangers. So I did my best to hide my fear and shame, and I convinced them to wait until the speaker was done. Once he finished, they darted to the van, giddy with excitement about the adventure ahead of them. Lucky for me, they didn't want me cramping their style or freaking people out with our sketchy 15-passenger van, so they asked me to just drop them off and maintain my distance while they went out to pray. As I sat in the van and watched them go, this feeling of pride in their bold faith washed over me. We didn't experience any "power encounters" that day, but they certainly had their faith expanded.

The next day, our flight home was delayed, and the whole group wanted to pray for people in the airport. I encouraged them to think through the implications of a post-9/11 airport experience for strangers, but as it turned out, I was forced to take a different, earlier flight home. I found out later that as soon as my flight took off, they started walking around the airport praying for people. So once again, I wasn't there to cramp their style, and they went out in boldness to share the love of Jesus with others.

Camps, conferences, retreats, and mission trips have a unique power to catalyze kids' faith and personal growth. Be strategic in the special events you expose them to. You don't even have to agree with everything you take your students to (sometimes the discussion after a session that you found questionable can be surprisingly fruitful), but you can use them to generate discussion, push the envelope, and stir things up.

CHAPTER CODA

A Haiku
God moves through even
The most pathetic (like me)
To shepherd his flock

EPILOGUE

Listen, we know it's tough to work with youth, and it can be really lonely and challenging sometimes. In a book written by Bob Goff a few years back (*Love Does*), he challenged us all to be more present and available to others. He even published his personal cell number in the back to model what that looks like. He really inspired us. And so, whenever you're stuck and in need of help, just give Bob a call—here's his number: 619-985-4747.

ACKNOWLEDGMENTS

It goes without saying, but we want to say it anyway: We owe a huge debt to a lot of people for the ideas and insights in this book. Very little except the stories is original. We owe a particular debt to the Rev. Whis Hays, Steven's youth ministry professor in seminary; and Dr. Dana Max, Psy D., PC, a former youth minister and licensed clinical psychologist from whom we borrowed most of the material in chapters four and five.

We'd like to thank those who took the time to read our manuscript and give us feedback: Luke Babbe, Ben Beasley, Erik Engstrom, Michael Goldstein, Julie Moser, Ross Neir, Ryan Rogers, Ellie Thomas, Heidi Thomas, Kaila Thomas, Tricia Tighe, Joanna Tong, Pieter Valk, and Dave Wright. And for expert review of our counseling chapters, Scott Pelking, a friend and licensed professional clinical counselor.